CONTENTS

CONTRIBUTORS

SEÁN FREYNE is Professor of Scripture at St Columban's College, Dalgan Park, Navan. Author of *The Twelve: Disciples and Apostles.*

GERARD WATSON is Professor of Classics, St Patrick's College, Maynooth. Author of *The Stoic Theory of Knowledge.*

P. J. MCGRATH is Professor of Metaphysics, St Patrick's College, Maynooth. Author of *The Nature of Moral Judgment.*

CIARAN RYAN is Lecturer in Mathematical Physics at University College, Dublin. Joint-author of *Theory of Weak Interactions.*

J. P. MACKEY is Professor of Dogmatic Theology at St John's College, Waterford. Author of *The Modern Theology of Tradition; Life and Grace; Tradition and Change in the Church.*

ENDA MCDONAGH is Professor of Moral Theology at St Patrick's College, Maynooth. Author of *Roman Catholics and Unity; The Declaration on Religious Freedom;* joint-author of *Truth and Life.*

PAUL SURLIS is Lecturer in Theology at St Patrick's College, Maynooth.

MORALS, LAW AND AUTHORITY

MORALS, LAW AND AUTHORITY

Sources and Attitudes in the Church

EDITED BY

J. P. MACKEY

GILL AND MACMILLAN   DUBLIN

First published 1969
Gill and Macmillan Ltd
2 Belvedere Place
Dublin 1

SBN 7171 0251 3

Nihil obstat: Laurentius Ryan, Censor Deputatus.

Imprimatur: +Patricius, Episcopus Kildarensis et Leighlinensis.
          3 May 1969.

The *Nihil obstat* and *Imprimatur* are a declaration that a book or periodical is considered to be free from doctrinal or moral error. This declaration does not imply approval of, or agreement with the contents, opinions or statements expressed.

Cover design by Des Fitzgerald

Printed and bound in the Republic of Ireland by the
Leinster Leader Ltd., Main Street, Naas, Co. Kildare.

INTRODUCTION

It would be disingenuous of us to pretend that there is no connection whatever between the publication of this book and the promulgation of the encyclical *Humanae Vitae*. The very timing of the publication, together with some similarity of subject matter, establishes a connection in any case. But it would be altogether unfair to the contributors to bracket this book with commentaries on that encyclical, and much more so to classify it in the category of internecine polemics. Many of the subjects had occupied the authors, and some of the material had even appeared in print, before *Humanae Vitae;* and the general viewpoint of the authors together with the range of topics covered by their contributions suggests a more general relevance than the immediate context of the *Humanae Vitae* debate could guarantee.

The fact that there is a peculiar ambivalence about the reception with which the more solemn kind of moral teaching by the Church meets cannot escape the notice of most thinking people and should raise some questions in their minds about that moral teaching. These more solemn pronouncements, particularly papal encyclicals and addresses, would seem to have had real authority and the greatest effect on people where least claims were made to absolute legal status for their contents. Consider, for instance, an encyclical like *Populorum Progressio*, the Pope's address to the United Nations, his constant imperative appeals for peace. These are all well received and have an effect for good; they do not meet with a strong reaction of dissent as happened in the case of *Humanae Vitae*. On the other hand, it is pronouncements that make absolute legal claims for their moral teaching that are most discussed and commented upon, as if they were the most important ones after all.

It is such ambivalence about the reception met with by contemporary moral pronouncements that should make us think at some depth about the Church as teacher or preacher of morals. This collection, then, aims at analysis in depth; by no means exhaustive, since each paper could be expanded into a book in its own right, but at least exploratory. The analysis concerns, in turn, the sources of moral teaching in the Church, the arguments by which it is recommended and the ideas and terms in which it is clothed, the manner in which it is imposed and received and, finally, the positive advantages which the Church can claim to possess in the moral quest of mankind.

Sources

It is perfectly clear from Freyne's article that the moral response is of the very essence of the covenant-relationship with God in the Old Testament and of the following of Christ in the New. Only the very best that man can do can be calculated to maintain and deepen his love-relationship with God. Yet Freyne's article shows how much the people of the Old Testament and the writers of the New were dependent on human research and human insights in order to discover the details of their moral response, the precepts and values by which they ought to govern their behaviour; correspondingly, how little of straightforward moral precept could be considered to have been revealed directly by God. One gets the impression that a great deal, if not the most substantial part, of the contribution of the Bible to morality is in the inspiration and motivation to moral endeavour that is there supplied. Certainly, the grace of another's forgiveness and love, the promise of richness and permanence from a new or restored relationship, is the best motivation and guidance to higher endeavours that a man can know. Yet there is always a danger, particular to moral theory and behaviour, that besets those who are conscious of being the chosen people of God, the danger, namely, of being tempted to impose detailed rules that will place too many burdens on too many people, of doing this in God's name, while not lifting a finger of their own to help, the danger of inflexibility, of legalism.

That the religious man does make use of the natural insights of human reason, indeed, that he is often influenced far more than he himself realizes by the moral codes and the general philosophical attitudes current in his age, and further, that this influence is not always beneficial to the true essence of Christianity, all this becomes rather disturbingly obvious in the course of Watson's contribution. He describes some of the general themes and attitudes of the pagan philosophers of Greece and Rome and one has only to read the descriptions in order to realize how much these have conditioned the Christian mind down to our own day.

There was, for instance, the Platonic belief in a realm of absolute, immutable truth or ideas, of which this world was a poor copy, which the philosopher could know and knowing should become king – in contrast to the Hegelian adage that has passed into so much of the *avant-garde* writing of our time: the truth is concrete. There was the gradual identification of this realm of ideas with the 'second God', the Logos or Word; there was the Stoic use of Logos for the rational order or law of nature, and the Christian use of the term 'Logos' for the second person of the Trinity. Combine these themes into one single, if confused, impression and, despite the difficulty, which even the pagans saw, of regarding a person at one and the same time as a law or rational system, one can see how Christians who knew Christ could come to conceive of themselves as having privileged access to an already constituted and immutable system of rational law which, as the new rulers of this world, they had to impose on the imperfect in order that things should become

better. Add the Roman reverence for promulgated law as practically the saviour of mankind; the picture is complete, then, and
its origins obvious.

Logic and Language

Once the impression is received that there is in existence an
immutable body of truth or law and that some group has privileged access to this, through special revelation to them or unique
illumination of their minds, there is a corresponding carelessness
about the evidence offered by this group or the arguments constructed by them in order to recommend any particular piece of
moral legislation. Never before in the history of the race have
men been so conscious of the evolutionary character of the
universe and, more particularly, of the role of man in changing
his world, in continually re-making himself and his world. Never
before has the idea of an already constituted and quite detailed
immutable moral law seemed less likely, though essential continuity of basic values and principles, based on a radical identity in human nature over the ages, is freely admitted. Yet the
idea of immutability in matters of fairly detailed legislation and
the idea of privileged access to details of an already existing
code do persist, and McGrath amply illustrates the carelessness
in production of evidence and construction of argument that
can ensue.

Inevitably this carelessness is calculated to make the worst
possible impression on those outside the Church who are otherwise seriously concerned with refinement of moral insight and
quite well disposed towards the efforts of the Church to bring
this about. As Ryan points out, the spokesmen for the Church
have regularly addressed themselves not simply to members of
the Church but to all men of good-will, and this practice is fully
in accord with the missionary nature of the Church. But it is not
only methods of argument that may provoke an unfavourable
reaction. Concepts and terms used can also prove an insur-
mountable barrier to this very essential type of missionary
communication.

Ryan is concerned with the scientific world which is familiar in its own way with the ideas and terminology of laws of nature. It is not simply the private mentality of the professional scientist that is in question here, with which communication at a certain stage becomes almost impossible. Much more, the sciences are valid and most progressive areas of human research, fully established for centuries now; they have, therefore, by reason of results achieved, the most profound influence on the reshaping of general philosophical thinking and, by reason of their popularity, not to say popularization, the most profound influence on the shaping of the general mentality of people of all classes and creeds. So, for instance, the scientific mentality is familiar with laws or regulations in nature, but as approximations more often than absolutes, and as discoveries to be manipulated for the benefit of man rather than norms for man's behaviour. To use the language that is familiar to this mentality while meaning something other than this is bound to seem like talking about some constructed picture of nature rather than the real one. A breakdown in communication is then the least unfortunate result that may be expected.

Imposition or Proposition

Besides such matters, the sources of the Church's moral teaching, the methods of argument and the concepts and terms used, there are other aspects of that teaching-in-practice that we felt needed some rethinking. Wherever its content is in fact found and however its conclusions are argued and phrased, how is the moral teaching of the Church proposed and how is it received?

I took it on myself to analyse that type of official Church teaching which is the one usually in evidence in the moral domain, the type which is designated authentic or authoritative, but not infallible, teaching. Though seldom, if ever, has a moral proposition been put forward with the specific claim to infallibility, it is nevertheless often the case that a moral teaching, though in theory admitted to be fallible and so reformable, is in

practice treated as if it were irreformable, at least until such
time has elapsed or such a volume of dissent arisen that this
position is simply no longer tenable. Thus authoritative teaching
is often treated in practice as a lesser form of infallible pronouncement. Then I suggest that authoritative pronouncements,
like those claimed to be infallible, must be issued and evaluated
with full consciousness of the differences that exist between the
realm of faith and the domain of morals. For, though there are
and must be authorities on morality in both civil and religious
societies, nevertheless, by reason of the very nature of the moral
quest and particularly of the truly moral response, the function
of what might be termed pure authority, the authority of 'it is to
be so because the leader has said so', is here minimal, when it
can be allowed at all, and it certainly cannot remain in force for
long either in the entire absence of reason or in the presence of
substantial contrary reasons.

McDonagh, in an article on conscience, looks on this same
aspect of moral teaching from the opposite point of view, not
how it is proposed, but how it should be received. In the after-
math of *Humanae Vitae* the subject of conscience was much in
vogue, but it is arguable that little advantage accrued to our
understanding of the subject as a result of this sudden notoriety.
Perhaps the reason some felt they had to take a hard line on
matters of conscience was the looseness with which certain epis-
copal statements allowed the appeal to conscience against the
Pope's decision (looseness, because they did not always make it
clear whether they held the Pope to be correct and thus were
only allowing the traditional rights to an *erroneous* conscience,
or whether, more likely in some cases at least, they were trying
to convey the impression that a contrary conscience, at least in
some situations, might conceivably be correct).

To say that one can expect approval only if one acts on an
informed conscience and then to say immediately that conscience
is informed by official teaching is to risk conveying an extremely
misleading impression. At least since the time of Aquinas it has
been commonplace in the Christian tradition to say that one

has the right to follow one's conscience, even against official or public legislation or philosophy, provided one has made every reasonable attempt to inform oneself fully on the matter in question. Naturally, the major factor in this attempt to inform oneself fully will be a most serious effort to understand and so to accept the official teaching of the Church. But to suggest that it is the official teaching of the Church alone that can properly inform the conscience is at once to deny that relative autonomy of conscience which the Christian tradition has so long explicitly recognized (see, for instance, E. D'Arcy, *Conscience and Its Right to Freedom,* London 1961, where this tradition is described and explained, for those who may be unaware of its existence), and to render all moral teaching of the Church in practice absolute and irreformable. Such a suggestion, in short, would be highly irresponsible.

It is the merit of McDonagh's contribution to suggest ways in which the understanding of the Christian conscience can be advanced even beyond this position, for he maintains, quite rightly, that it has not advanced much since the Middle Ages. He suggests that conscience should be seen to involve the whole person, not just his practical intellect; the person reacting from within himself to the full reality of God and world proposed to him and seen by him, rather than reacting as a subject of laws imposed too much from without; a person in dynamic interaction with the community that at once fashions him and yet anticipates his own unique, individual contribution. In such a vastly richer theology of conscience the true freedom and responsibility, the truly unique contribution of each individual begins to appear, something of which the phrase 'private judgement' is but an inconsiderate caricature.

Positive Perspectives

It is the task of the final essay, by Surlis, to indicate the real (rather than imaginary), unique advantages which the Church possesses and, consequently, the true nature of the contribution it can make towards the advance of good moral living. For instance, the Church is the privileged bearer of belief in a creating and guiding God, a belief that lends a foundation of meaningfulness to life, without which further search for meaning by individuals or peoples in their own places and times is likely largely to fail. The Church believes that once evil-doing entered human history it increased until it conditioned mankind to evil, so much so that only the inspiration of divine love in human form – a love at once forgiving, practical, individual and fully human – could rouse man to the inhumanity of so many of his pursuits and guide him to more human, i.e. more moral, behaviour. The lived example of such unlimited love as is seen in the life of Christ is the greatest spur to moral advancement that man can know, precisely because it is not and cannot be contained in any single legal or social system, though it always commends to us the best of these. Finally, because of Christ the Church carries the hope of resurrection, which reiterates the goodness of all things created by God and to be created by us, since resurrection is a continuing of God's creativity, and which brings us the motivation that only promise of permanence can bring.

The Church's main contribution even to morality, then, is still to preach the great central truths of the faith without flagging, and to continually draw out their implications. Already in this there is foundation, inspiration and guidance towards better human living. God's love for individuals leads towards rules of behaviour in which the good of the individual is the true value; God's acknowledged fatherhood of all men inspires men to work for the whole family of man, the peace of the whole and the sustenance of even the most distant branches. The Church will spell out, as it has always done, the principles by which men's behaviour must be guided, but by its very nature it will always want to go beyond existing codes; it will draw as much response as possible from individual creative conscience, rather than impose detailed rules without care for inequalities of character and opportunity on simply obedient subjects; it will hold up the great ideals of love, justice, peace and generosity and put more trust in men to work out the detailed systems or codes in which these can be successively achieved. Faithful to a persistent theme in the parables of its founder, the Church will try to provide the leaven for society which works almost imperceptibly from hidden places in the hearts of men, rather than try to provide a container that would impose a rigid form on society.

This volume cannot work out in detail how the Church ought to behave in matters of moral promulgation, but perhaps the passages to which Surlis refers from the documents of the Council, together with reflection on the reception which some pronouncements received when others did not, might provide practical guidance over a terrain of Church policy that in our time still remains to be mapped out clearly.

J. P. MACKEY

SEÁN FREYNE

THE BIBLE AND CHRISTIAN MORALITY

In recent times all Catholic theology has had a *crise de conscience* concerning its use of the Bible. Centuries of a tape-and-scissors use in theology manuals has given way to a more accurate determination of the meaning of the Scripture text in the light of historical and literary criticism. But this growing awareness of the need for more refined handling of the Bible by theologians does not always have positive results. Texts no longer say what they appear to say and the overall impression is one of frustration if not futility in this task of relating Scripture to theology. A new approach is called for, one that can do full justice to the exigencies of biblical science and yet has something fruitful to offer theologians as they grapple with contemporary problems. This essay offers the opportunity for such an approach.

One cannot hope to give a detailed treatment of the whole topic of biblical morality. I propose instead to take the Bible as reflecting the beliefs, attitudes and manners of the people of the covenant, the people of faith. In it I hope to discover a record of how this people of faith approached the problem of moral living throughout the various circumstances of its history from the Mesopotamia of Abraham to the Rome of Paul. Looking at the Bible in this way one is not so concerned with specific contents of biblical morality, since one can readily recognize the time

1

conditioned character of much of it. Rather I try to discover what was distinctive about the approach of the people of the Bible to morality. How did faith determine and enlighten its conduct; how much better off is it than its neighbours in discovering how man should lead the good life and in what that good life consists? Such a use of the Bible in theology seems to me to best take account of its historical and time-conditioned nature, on the one hand, and yet accept its normative value as God's word for the Church of every age, on the other.

One could answer the question of what is distinctive about biblical morality briefly by saying that it regards man's behaviour as the direct and immediate response to God's revealed will. On page after page of the Old Testament Yahweh is introduced as the ultimate source of and the sole justification for the conduct that is being demanded from his people. Of course this does not mean that biblical morality is not interested in the dignity of one's fellow man but such an interest is based on the fact that, as part of God's creation, all men enjoy a communal relation of friendship with their creator. In the New Testament God's revealed will has become incarnate in Christ and so the New Testament writers constantly draw attention to the pattern of his earthly life, and his present demands as glorified Lord on those who believe in him, when proposing to them a way of life that is Christian.

Such a general answer opens the way to two further questions which will serve as directions for this essay. Firstly, if biblical morality is concerned with God's revealed will, one immediately asks how is this will revealed to Israel, and how did she discover it? Does Israel consider herself as having an immediate access to this will by contrast with the other nations, and if so, does this dispense her from involving herself in the historical discovery of what that will entails? Secondly and relatedly, how does Yahweh's will impose itself on Israel and how does man consider himself bound by it?

In speaking of Israel here we do not confine ourselves to the people of the Old Testament merely, but include also the people of the new covenant. The name Israel describes the religious reality that is God's people, and equally well applies to the Christian community, for Christ did not form a new people, but rather he established a new covenant with God's people. In other words there is a basic unity in the people of the Bible, both Old and New Testament, something that is fully recognized by Christ and the New Testament writers after him.

A consideration of the two questions just outlined is of immediate interest to current discussions on morality. If we find that God's people in its formative period has a particular approach to thinking about the good life and the way it proposes this to the man of faith, then clearly the Church of every other age must treat its moral problems in a similar way. Only then is God's will in leaving the Scriptures to the Church as the source of its life and faith, fully respected.

I. The Content of Biblical Morality

A reading of the historical books of the Old Testament gives on the whole a unified picture of Israel's origins, her period of slavery in Egypt and her entry into the promised land. However, historical and literary criticism has shown that this unity is theological rather than historical. Archaeology has shed new light on the varied social conditions of Israel's ancestors of the patriarchal period;[1] the exodus from Egypt may well have involved several separate and unconnected revolts against Egyptian tyranny, the accounts of which were later fused together within the common stream of Israel's faith;[2] the taking possession

1. The studies of R. de Vaux are fundamental in this area. Originally there were three articles: 'Les Patriarches Hébraux et les découvertes modernes', *Revue Biblique* (43) 1946, 321-47; (45) 1948, 321-47; (46) 1949, 5-36. These have now been summarized and brought up to date in *Theology Digest* (12) 1964, 227-40.

2. This conclusion is based on literary criticism of the Pentateuch and the discovery of various independent traditions concerning the departure from Egypt and entry into Palestine. See e.g. the studies of M. Noth, *Überlieferungsgeschichte des Pentateuchs,* Stuttgart 1948; *The History of Israel,* London 1960, 110-20.

of Palestine appears to have been the outcome of a long and involved process of settlement rather than the result of a united military onslaught as described in the book of Joshua.[3] Such heterogeneity of origin and social background is clearly reflected in the various laws and customs that we find being presented in one block as God's will for his covenant people in later Israel. This code of behaviour for day to day living has, when examined, all the marks of its origin within the social and cultural milieu of the ancient Near East, and this would seem to indicate that Israel like any other nation discovered it there experientially from the demands of life in that setting. In other words, faith and revelation has not taken early Israel out of its historical setting or rendered the human search for such a code unnecessary or superfluous.

Early Israel

It is well known that there are two different forms of law in the Pentateuch, apodeictic and casuistic. According to the classic study by Albrecht Alt[4] the former is unique in Israel and we shall discuss its significance presently. On the other hand, the casuistic form, i.e. that which proposes a law from the starting point of a particular case, is widespread in the other legal systems of that epoch and region. The Code of Hammurabi (c. 1700 B.C.) from Babylon, for example, is really a collection of such casuistic laws. Thus Israel, for these laws at least, draws on a common tradition, or better is part of a common tradition that determines both the form and the content of her ethical system.

Many of the customs from the pre-Mosaic period, as, for example, a barren wife accepting as heir the child her husband has by a slave girl (*Gen.* 15:1-4), or possession of household gods giving the right of inheritance (*Gen.* 31:19-35), have been paralleled by the discoveries in Mesopotamia dating from the

3. See Noth, *The History of Israel*, 53-109.
4. *Die Ürsprunge des israelitischen Rechts*, Leipzig 1934; reprinted in *Essays in Old Testament History and Religion*, Oxford 1966, 81-132.

second millenium B.C. The oldest collection of casuistic laws in the Pentateuch is the so-called Book of the Covenant (*Exod.* 21:1 – 23:19). This collection probably dates from the time when Israel was already in possession of the land, that is from the early monarchical period, but form critical analysis shows that some at least of its contents date from much earlier. It differs from the two later codes of Deuteronomy and the Holiness code (*Lev.* 16-26), in that it contains very little religious motivation, and is more like a collection of purely secular laws. (See however, *Exod.* 22:21-27; 23:9.) Even a casual glance at these laws, dealing with slavery, property rights, money lending etc. makes it clear that they have to do with everyday occurrences of town (e.g. *Exod.* 22:24) and country (e.g. *Exod.* 21:37) life. The tone throughout is for the most part utilitarian, as is evidenced, for example, in this description of the Sabbath law (*Exod.* 23:12): 'For six days you shall do your work, but stop on the seventh day, so that your ox and your donkey may rest, and the son of your slave girl may have a breathing space'. (Contrast the religious motivation based on the story of creation, *Exod.* 20:8-11.) Clearly therefore, this is popular morality derived from varied circumstances and backgrounds and introduced now into a covenant setting.

The question must now be asked to what extent this popular morality is more refined in Israel than among her neighbours? Clearly, a detailed survey is outside the limits of this study, but some general observations seem pertinent. One notices that the Israelite casuistic law is not as detailed or extensive as the Code of Hammurabi or the Assyrian code. This could mean that many areas were left to the moral sense of individuals or clans with faith in a just and moral God Yahweh as a basis for mutual trust and respect. It would seem also that there was greater respect for human life in Israel: thus property offences do not carry the death penalty; slaves are to be protected from inhuman abuse (*Exod.* 21.20, 26 f.); bodily mutilations as punishment for certain crimes are missing, with the exception of Deuteronomy 25:11 f. There is no class distinction in the administration of Israelite justice and in fact widows and orphans are given express protection by the law (*Exod*. 22:22 f.).

In all these examples it would seem that faith in Yahweh, the God who had liberated Israel from the slavery of Egypt, before whom all are equal, since all are created by him, had the effect of achieving a more refined moral sense. However, this conclusion based on general observations, can yield to contrary proof. The Code of Hammurabi gives to wives many rights which are not mentioned in Israel in regard to divorce, debts incurred by her husband etc. She is therefore given greater protection by the law. Eichrodt sees this merely as a sign of a more highly developed urban life by comparison with the rural and clan civilization in Israel.[5] This may indeed be so, but it still shows that revelation alone did not determine the formal content of Israel's ethical code, or free her from the obligation of purifying her popular morality through the centuries, prompted even by contacts with her pagan neighbours; and that the moral code of the people of faith can in some respects lag behind that of others at least in its explicit formulation.

The Decalogue is the best known group of apodeictic laws (i.e. 'you shall ...' and 'you shall not ...') in the Pentateuch (*Exod*. 20:1-17; *Deut*. 5:6-21), but there is evidence of similar lists at Deuteronomy 27:15-26; Leviticus 19:11-18; Exodus 21; 12:15-17. To understand the function of such lists it is important to give them their true setting in the cultic life of the people, as can be seen, for example, from Psalm 81. The introduction of this psalm clearly indicates its processional tone on the occasion of the new moon festival; it then goes on to recall Israel's wanderings in the desert, and finally through the psalmist Yahweh proclaims the first commandment to the assembly: there shall be no strange gods among you (verse 9). Probably the whole Decalogue was recited at such gatherings at the central sanctuary when the community re-dedicated itself to Yahweh.[6]

5. See W. Eichrodt, *Theology of the Old Testament* (E. tr.), I, London 1961, 81.

6. See Alt, *Essays ...*, 123 f.

In the book of Joshua, chapter 24 describes one such ceremony in which the Sinai covenant is renewed. Recent analysis of this chapter has discovered beneath the present Deuteronomic redaction an earlier narrative of a gathering, in which the tribes who had not shared in the exodus experience were offered a share in the covenant with Yahweh by Joshua and his house.[7] In all probability tribal law determined conduct at the local level, but it was necessary to have some statement of what belief in the common god, Yahweh, demanded of all Israel, and such lists as the Decalogue indicated the various areas in which Yahweh's will was absolute. Seen in this light one can understand the negative form of most of the commandments, which was prob- ably the form of all originally. They do not attempt to prescribe a total ethical system for Israel, but rather describe what was absolutely displeasing to Yahweh. As von Rad puts it: 'If then these commandments do not subject life to a comprehensive normative law, it is more appropriate for us to say that in cer- tain marginal situations they demand avowal of Yahweh, and this avowal consists precisely in abstaining from doing certain things displeasing to him'.[8]

Once we see the Decalogue in this covenant context as describ- ing the minimum requirements which faith in Yahweh demanded, we shall never be tempted to regard it as a set of immutable principles from which a detailed moral code can be derived. Certainly Israel did not consider it to be such, as can be seen from the existence of several different lists, and the additions and changes which they all underwent in the course of the cen- turies. Besides, as we have seen, the Book of the Covenant (*Exod*. 21-23), with its detailed prescriptions, was in later times set side by side with the Decalogue (*Exod*. 20). This shows that Israel felt the need to spell out the moral obligations of the covenant people far beyond the situations described by or con- tained in the Decalogue. By thus introducing popular morality, derived as we have seen from various sources and backgrounds,

7. See J. L. McKenzie, *The World of the Judges,* London 1967, 68-71.
8. G. von Rad, *Old Testament Theology* (E. tr.), I, London 1962, 195.

into the covenant context, Israel was saying that her faith assured her that she was doing Yahweh's will in her moral behaviour. She was also recognizing that the covenant grace did not dispense her from discovering that will historically.

The Prophets

All modern study of the prophets recognizes that they share in the mainstream of Israel's religious tradition, and are concerned with the people's faithlessness to the God who saved them from Egypt. We cannot regard law and prophets as two mutually opposed religious forces in Israel, as some earlier critics have attempted to do.[9] This can be shown, among other ways, from a consideration of the prophets' castigation of Israel's moral failures. They see them as failures to observe the covenant law, and the curses that were the punishment for such failures in the covenant context (e.g. *Deut.* 27), can now be re-interpreted in terms of God's judgements against Israel. Thus the prophet Nathan confronts David with his violation of the commandments on adultery and murder in arranging for the death of Uriah in battle because he desired his wife, Bathsheba (2 *Sam.* 12). The divine judgement inherent in the law is manifested in this instance by the death of the child who is the offspring of this unlawful union. Elijah likewise confronts the king Ahab and Jezebel, his wife, for taking possession of Nathan's property in direct violation of the Decalogue (1 *Kings* 21). The curse is to fall on Ahab's son, Joram, according to the prophet; and when he was actually put to death by Jehu all Israel remembered Elijah's word (2 *Kings* 9:26).

The example of these two early prophets is carried on by the later writing prophets. One finds in these a repeated appeal to a collection of apodeictic laws like those of the Decalogue in order to confront Israel with her moral failures: 'Hear the word of the Lord, O people of Israel; for the Lord has a controversy with the inhabitants of the land. There is no faithfulness or kindness,

9. See W. Zimmerli, *The Law and the Prophets, A Study in the Meaning of the Old Testament*, Oxford 1965.

and no knowledge of God in the land; there is swearing, lying, killing, stealing and committing adultery; they break all bounds and murder follows murder' (*Hos.* 4:1 f.; cf. also *Jer.* 7:1-11; *Ezek.* 22:6-12).

The striking condemnation of the social ills of his day by the prophet Amos is clearly based on certain prescriptions of the Book of the Covenant relating to unjust treatment of the poor, taking of garments as pledges and taking interest on loans granted to the needy (*Exod.* 22:21 f., 25, 26 f.). These are all specifically mentioned by the prophet as he castigates the rich of the northern kingdom (*Amos* 2:6; 3:10; 5:11; 8:4-8).

In laying so much stress on Israel's failures to observe the law of Yahweh the prophets were making a very important clarification in regard to the nature of her response. Cultic worship meant little to Yahweh as long as his people refused genuine worship of the heart by a life lived in fidelity to the covenant law.[10] The poignant outbursts of Amos, 'I hate, I despise your feasts, and I take no delight in your solemn assemblies' (*Amos* 5:21-24), is re-echoed by all subsequent prophets: Hosea 6:6; Jeremiah 7:21-23; Isaiah 1:11-17; Micah 6:6-8. More than anything else what Yahweh required from his people was the worship of an upright life: 'Wash yourselves; make yourselves clean; remove the evil you are doing from before my eyes; cease to do evil, learn to do good; seek justice, correct oppression; defend the fatherless, plead for the widow' (*Is.* 1:16 f.; cf. *Amos* 5:15).

We must understand this apparent opposition to the cult precisely in the light of its failure to motivate the people to observe the law, which, we have seen, had its original home within the cult at the great yearly gatherings of all the tribes at the central sanctuary. Thus the prophets clearly recognize where Israel's primary responsibility lies, and their major contribution to moral thinking consists in highlighting its absolutely funda-

10. R. E. Clements has shown this in his excellent study of the prophets' contribution to the covenant community, *Prophecy and Covenant*, London 1965.

mental importance in the covenant relationship between Yahweh and his people.

However, it must be stated that the prophetic movement also contributed greatly to a refinement of Israel's moral sense through the centuries.[11] The more the nation's leaders took a path which led to connivance with foreign powers and ignoring of Yahweh as the director of Israel's destiny, the more the prophets realized that Israel's future as God's people could never lie in great political success. War and the virtues associated with it are no longer a sacred duty as in the earlier period, but are seen to belong to the secular sphere, and even as opposed to God's will. Instead the emphasis is on building up the nation internally through care and concern for the needy and oppressed. These are the special concern of Yahweh, the faithful shepherd of his oppressed flock (*Is.* 7:7 f.; 17:12 f.; *Jer.* 25:15 f.; *Ezek.* 25 etc.). Conformity to Yahweh's will demands the same kind of interest in the afflicted within the community of Israel. Thus an ethic of suffering emerges, and arrogance and power are no longer signs of Yahweh's favour. The ideal he looks for is rather humble submission to life's disappointments, for it is to his *anawîm* that he grants his mercy (*Amos* 2:6-7; *Is.* 3:14-15; *Jer.* 5:28 etc.).[12]

Clearly then, the prophets' contribution to moral teaching in Israel is not based on any special revelation of content from God. Rather, they refined the traditional morality in certain respects, and they stressed the centrality of good moral living, however its details were discovered, in the Israelite's response to the God who had so graciously approached him.

The Wisdom Literature

The Wisdom literature is of special importance for our enquiry since it is largely concerned with the good life. Once again, more important than the actual content is the way in

11. W. Eichrodt, *Theology of the Old Testament* (E. tr.), II, London 1967, 326-37.

12. See A. Gelin, *The Poor of Yahweh* (E. tr.), Collegeville 1963.

which the Wisdom tradition, with its secular and extra-Israelite origins, came to be accepted as part of all Israel's religious inheritance. This only happened, of course, in the post-exilic community of the law in the wake of the disillusionment of the high hopes at the return from Babylon. The emphasis came to be placed more and more on the problems of everyday living rather than on any immediate hope of a decisive intervention by Yahweh in favour of his people.[13] The older Wisdom material is pressed into service of the law, so that gradually scribe and wisdom teacher come to be identified, as in the writings of Ben Sirach *(Ecclesiasticus,* c. 190 B.C.), for example. Originally, this tradition had flourished outside Israel, mainly in court circles, so that the recollection that it was Solomon who introduced wisdom to Israel is probably correct, for we know that he organized the court on Egyptian lines.[14] All through the period of the monarchy the relations between the prophets and wisdom teachers are strained, for the latter often advise the reigning king in a way that seems to ignore Israel's firm belief in Yahweh as the only guide for the nation that is his people *(Is.* 10:13; 29:14-16; *Jer.* 8:8 f.).[15]

In the post-exilic period, therefore, many maxims and insights that had been discovered outside Israel were used in the service of her faith. In particular the 'older wisdom', as von Rad calls it, that is found in Proverbs, was fashioned through reflection on the experiences of life and the enigmas which these posed.[16] In Egypt such maxims were often concerned with achieving a successful life at court, but in the religious sphere they have a very different perspective. Avoidance of greed, selfishness or opportunism are important for a young man if he would succeed

13. See J. Bright, *A History of Israel,* London 1960, 413-45.
14. See the articles of M. Noth, N. W. Porteus and R. B. Y. Scott in *Wisdom in Israel and the Ancient Near East,* edited by M. Noth and D. W. Thomas, Leiden 1960 (Essays presented to H. H. Rowley).
15. See J. Lindblom, 'Wisdom in the Old Testament Prophets', in *Wisdom in Israel ...,* 192-204.
16. *Old Testament Theology,* I, 418-41.

in life, but motivated by Israel's faith they become expressions of the values of justice, respect for one's neighbour and trust in the God who guides all men's destinies, qualities that are so dear to Yahweh.[17]

The Wisdom tradition is based on experience of life and therefore strives to inculcate respect for the elders in society. Transferred to the religious context this means that the family virtues and esteem for parents are regarded as important, and this makes it a useful commentary on the Decalogue:

> With all your heart honour your father,
> Never forget the birthpangs of your mother.
> Remember that you owe your birth to them;
> How can you repay them for what they have done for you?
> (*Sir.* 7:27-30)

If a young man wishes to win the confidence of the great ones at court honesty is of paramount importance for him, but this too, is a quality that the Decalogue had demanded from the genuine Israelite:

> Where hatred is, there are dissembling lips,
> but deep within lies treachery;
> The lying tongue hates the truth,
> the fawning mouth brings ruin (*Prov.* 26:24, 28).

A detailed examination of the whole material is clearly outside the scope of this essay, but these examples may help to show how Israel in the hour of religious need, caused by the apparent failure of her salvation history, could call on such natural insights as those of the Wisdom tradition and use them to deepen the awareness and understanding of Yahweh's will for his community.

17. In this regard compare the 'Instruction of Amen-em-Opet' from Egypt (in J. B. Pritchard, *Ancient Near Eastern Texts*, New Jersey 1950, 421-4) with *Prov.* 22:17 – 24:22.

Jesus

In discussing the ethical teaching of Jesus, even in outline, it is important to see it against the background of developments in the late Jewish period. It is only thus, by the principle of dissimilarity, as it is called, that we can really determine the originality of Jesus.[18] At the same time we must try to distinguish his own teaching from later adaptation and development by the apostolic community, for form criticism has certainly shown that the words of Jesus were applied to new situations and problems within the life of the post-Easter community.

There are a number of attitudes in late Jewish moral thinking to which Jesus is clearly opposed.[19] In the first place the law had been absolutized to such a degree that each and every part had equal binding authority on the individual, and this was true not just for the written torah, but also for the crop of oral prescriptions that the scribes had built up around it. This meant that moral, ritual and cultic laws all had equal binding force, and only occasionally did individual Rabbis attempt to grade them in importance. Despite the great multiplicity of laws there were still many areas that were not covered explicitly. This meant that people who had been conditioned to look for detailed guidance tended to adopt a neutral or indifferent attitude in the absence of any positive binding directive. Certain good works such as prayers, fastings and almsgiving were indeed recognized beyond the sphere of duty, but performance of these works of supererogation was considered to entitle a person to special rewards from God, an attitude that easily led to self-sufficiency and complacency. It would be inaccurate to suggest that the late Jewish ethic was solely motivated by the idea of reward however, but the dominant theme still was absolute obedience

18. See N. Perrin, *Rediscovering the Teaching of Jesus,* London 1967, especially ch. 1.

19. For a summary account of the position see W. D. Davies, 'Law in first-century Judaism', in *The Interpreter's Dictionary of the Bible*, III, New York 1955, 89-95.

to the supreme authority of the law, and to this in particular Jesus was opposed.

In discussing the teaching of Jesus one must begin with his proclamation of the kingdom of God, present in and with his own person. The phrase 'the kingdom of God' refers, not to territory or to overlordship in the secular sense, but to man's acceptance of the God who graciously approached him, and to man's consequent adherence to a certain way of life. It was Christ who demonstrated what this acceptance meant and what this way of life was. This was the central point of his mission as he understood it, and accordingly his teaching on morality, with regard to both content and motivation, was based on it.[20] We shall return to the question of motivation in the second part of this paper, but it is necessary to refer to it here also since it helps to draw attention to the main concern of Jesus, namely, to live out God's kingdom and its demands to the full in his own life and teaching. He was thereby giving a pattern of behaviour in accord with the nature of the kingdom, on which he could base his authoritative call to men to follow him.

In external form he and his group must have appeared like any typical Rabbi-disciple group of contemporary Palestine, but it is clear that his consciousness of himself and his mission was much more that of the longed-for one who finally realized salvation in Israel.[21] Accordingly the ethical teaching of Jesus cannot be regarded as an *Interimsethik*, as has been maintained in the past.[22] It is no irksome burden that man can tolerate because the end is near, nor is it merely ascetical preparation for the coming of the kingdom. On the other hand Jesus makes

20. The relation between the moral teaching of Jesus and his preaching of the kingdom has been well presented by R. Schnackenburg, in his two studies *Gottes Herrschaft und Reich* Freiburg 1959, and *Die Sittliche Botschaft des Neuen Testamentes*, Munich 1962.

21. I have discussed this aspect of Jesus's ministry in *The Twelve: Disciples and Apostles*, London 1968, ch. 1.

22. For a discussion of the views of A. Schweitzer and J. Weiss who pioneered the idea see the survey of N. Perrin, *The Kingdom of God in the Teaching of Jesus*, London 1963, 16-28.

it clear that we can never merit the kingdom: 'When you have done all that is commanded you say: "we are unworthy servants; we have done what is our duty" ' (*Luke* 17:7-10). Yet once we accept the kingdom as God's gift we must act in accordance with its urgent demands, making full use of all the talents given (*Matt.* 25:14-30). By receiving the kingdom we gain forgiveness of our sins, the cancellation of the great debt (*Matt.* 18:23-34), and yet we are to pray for the growing experience of this forgiveness (Our Father). This in turn increases our sense of forgiveness for our fellow-man. In other words, the grace of the kingdom once received makes demands on us that correspond with its own nature.[23] Little wonder then that we find such expressions as 'receiving the kingdom' or 'entering the kingdom' side by side with others like 'doing the will of my Father' or 'follow me' as general descriptions of the moral behaviour which Jesus expected of all those who listened to his gospel of the kingdom.

Once we make his proclamation of the kingdom our starting point we are in a better position to understand where the emphasis lies in the teaching of Jesus. He was particularly concerned that men should understand the true nature of the kingdom and it would seem that this was one of the issues on which he was put to death. It is significant that the parables of Jesus, dealing as they do with the true nature of the kingdom, are much more original than his specific moral pronouncements, when both are contrasted with contemporary Jewish sources.[24] We need not expect from Jesus a fully worked out moral system similar to those already existing in Judaism. Indeed his con-

23. See J. Jeremias, 'Le Sermon sur la Montagne', in *Paroles de Jésus*, Paris 1963, 16-48.

24. This point has been illustrated by W. R. Farmer, 'An Historical Essay on the Humanity of Jesus Christ', in *Christian History and Interpretation: Studies Presented by John Knox,* edited by W. R. Farmer, C. F. D. Moule, R. R. Niebuhr, Cambridge 1967, 101-26. Farmer gives detailed parallels to the sayings of Jesus, especially those of the Sermon on the Mount, from the rabbinical writings, and also some examples of contemporary parables.

demnation of the Pharisees seems to centre precisely on this that by their detailed system they made it impossible for 'the people' to enter the kingdom (*Matt.* 23:13). Such a condemnation is all the more necessary when we hear Rabbi Hillel declare: 'There is no uneducated man (i.e. no one not a scribe) who fears sin. Not one of "the people of the land" (i.e. the common people) is religious.' In this connection too it is interesting to note that the Qumran covenanters had set themselves an ideal of perfection consisting of observance not only of the law but of all the community rules besides. For Jesus on the other hand perfection meant acceptance of the kingdom and its demands, following the pattern of his own life (*Matt.* 5:48; 19:21).[25] And, of course, as Bultmann rightly maintains, we can certainly not expect to find in Jesus's teaching a system of ethics dealing with standards of behaviour or moral values, which would correspond with the Greek idea of a life of virtue, and is quite foreign to the Semitic way of thinking.[26]

At the same time we find that Jesus engaged himself in Jewish discussions about morality, even if these were thrust on him by those who held official positions. His new attitude is not that of an iconoclastic revolutionary with regard to Jewish institutions. Some have gone so far as to suggest that he adopted two different attitudes to the law which can scarcely be made to correspond: sometimes ignoring it, sometimes dealing in almost the same kind of casuistry as Pharisaism. This impression may well be due to the fact that it is to St Matthew's gospel in particular that we must turn for the fullest account of Jesus's teaching on these matters. Matthew paints a conservative picture of Jesus's attitude to Jewish law (*Matt.* 5:17-19), yet it must be recognized that in all probability this gospel was written within a polemical situation in the Jewish Christian wing of the early Church, and may therefore be more conservative than Jesus in

25. See my *The Twelve* ..., 160, note 2.
26. See *Jesus and the Word,* Fontana Books, 1958, 66 f. (this is a translation of his famous study *Jesus,* Berlin 1929.)

regard to the law.[27] At all events we would do well to cross-check our conclusions from the other sources for the teaching of Jesus, Mark and Q. That Jesus should discuss the ethical implications of his proclamation within the categories of Jewish moral thinking, is only another way of saying that his earthly mission was in the main directed to Israel (*Matt.* 15:24). He saw himself as heir to all that the God of the fathers had done for his people as found in the law and the prophets, and there could be no question of abandoning that inheritance. Yet a new interpretation of the demands that Yahweh's loving kindness made on his people seemed called for in the light of what he was doing in and through Jesus.

In the first place it seems certain that Jesus rejected the formal authority of the Scriptures as absolutely binding. He does not hesitate to interpret the Scriptures for his contemporaries not as a scribe who spells out their every implication, but as one who can oppose one passage to another and show how they correspond with God's kingdom in the present. On the divorce question, for example, Genesis 1:27; 2:24 are set over against Deuteronomy 24:1 (*Mark* 10:2-9 and par.), thereby explaining what the original will of God was. Scripture is still authoritative, but it must be read in the light of God's final intervention which is to restore things as they were in the beginning, and not be interpreted in any literalistic manner. Even more sweeping is Jesus's condemnation of the Jewish ritual law. It is the heart of man that is important, as the prophets had previously insisted, and ritual prescriptions cannot determine man's total acceptance or rejection of God (*Mark* 7:14 f.). The precise gospel formulations of this attitude of Jesus are so clear that for some the subsequent struggle in the Church is difficult to explain, if Jesus had pronounced so definitively on the matter. And yet these

27. R. Hummel, *Die Auseinandersetzung zwischen Kirche und Judentum im Matthäusevangelium*, Munich 1963, 34-71. Also G. Barth, 'Matthew's Understanding of the Law', in G. Bornkamm, G. Barth and H. J. Held, *Tradition and Interpretation in Matthew* (E. tr.), London 1960, 159-65.

formulations of his attitude can only be based on Jesus's whole
practice and on his associations with Gentiles and sinners during
the ministry, something that cannot be denied in view of the
amount of evidence in the tradition.[28] Jesus also rejected any
legalistic interpretation of the Sabbath command – 'The Sabbath was made for man, not man for the Sabbath' (*Mark* 2:27).

Questions which are sometimes posed to Jesus, such as:
'Which is the greatest commandment?' (*Mark* 12:28 and par.),
or 'What shall I do to obtain eternal life?' (*Mark* 10:17 and
par.) were often discussed in rabbinic circles, and the fact that
Jesus is prepared to discuss these shows that he does not reject
the idea of the Jewish search for the good life, even if he cannot
answer them on conventional lines. The rich young man who
had observed the Decalogue from his youth is not far from the
kingdom, but he must imitate the total abandonment of Jesus.
The greatest commandment is the love commandment, but this
is universalized in line with Jesus's own attitude towards all
that come to him in his ministry, something that again is in
striking contrast to the Qumran community's attitude of love
for the brother and hatred for all those who lived outside the
community.[29]

Much has sometimes been made of the fact that many of the
specific instructions of Jesus, such as those of the Sermon on
the Mount, can be paralleled from the rabbinical sources. Bultmann, for example, sees in this a sign that we cannot expect
Jesus to formulate concrete requirements or indicate an attitude
towards concrete ethical problems.[30] But this is to adopt a much
too one-sided approach and to place all the stress on Jesus as
the eschatological prophet of the kingdom calling for an immediate decision from men. This aspect is indeed central as we
have seen, but Jesus is also a teacher whose words are remembered and regarded as authoritative, precisely because of his

28. C. E. Carlston, 'The Things that Defile (*Mark* 7:14) and the Law
in Matthew and Mark', *New Testament Studies* (15) 1968-9, 75-95.
29. Schnackenburg, *Die Sittliche Botschaft*, 65-71.
30. *Jesus and the Word*, 68.

eschatological proclamation. Once we accept that Jesus can combine these two roles, prophet and teacher, in his own person, what is striking is his agreement with and acceptance of the better insights and formulations of the late Jewish moral thinking. Even here at the very climax of God's revelation of his will to man he can and does translate the one fundamental command, acceptance of the kingdom or obedience, into areas of current concern. In doing so Jesus used the insights that he found before him, adding to them now the authority of the one who spoke them. As Davies puts it: 'The acts and words of Jesus compel the same question. They belong together as part of the ethic of Jesus and the mystery of his person: his words themselves confront us with him who utters them.'[31]

Jesus's basic request to men was to 'follow me', to imitate the selfless pattern of his life; this rather than spell out a detailed moral code for them. Hence his definitive contribution belongs more to the second section of this paper, and the Johannine writings, as we shall see in that section, are correct when they put forward Jesus's moral teaching chiefly in terms of the command to love, spelled out mainly in concrete terms of forgiveness, practical caring and unlimited self-sacrifice. As far as codified law is concerned, Jesus inherited and refined rather than innovated.

The Apostolic Church

Our interpretation of the approach of Jesus to morality is borne out by the great variety of moral argumentation to be found in the apostolic communities which are grounded on his life and ministry. Here we can only indicate some examples which show that these communities never considered that they had received a complete code of morality to deal with every situation. The pattern which we discovered earlier in relation to the Old Testament recurs here: the community of faith must

31. W. D. Davies, *The Setting of the Sermon on the Mount*, Cambridge 1964, 433. See the full discussion, 425-35, for a valid critique of Bultmann's position.

discover what its moral response should be in the face of specific moral problems; in doing so it can call on contemporary approaches to such problems, bringing these into line with its understanding of the Lord and the demands he is making on those who have followed him.

Clearly the words of Jesus had an authoritative value, not merely for those who actually heard them but also after his death and resurrection. Occasionally Paul can call explicitly on the 'word of the Lord' to answer a particular problem (1 *Thess.* 4:14 f.; 1 *Cor.* 7:10, 14, 25; 9:14). More often, however, he appeals to the mind of the master by an implicit reference to his words as they are known to us from the gospel tradition.[32] This use of the words of Jesus is not confined to Paul, since it is generally recognized that the epistle of James has also used them quite frequently (e.g. *Jas.* 2:5, 13, 15; 3:12, 18; 5:10, 12). The collection of sayings of Jesus usually designated as Q would also appear to have been compiled for moral instruction in a catechetical milieu.[33] All this is in line with what form criticism has told us about the transmission of the words of Jesus in the oral period.

There is no rigid adherence to the letter of what the master said, for the early Christian teachers, least of all Paul, cannot be regarded as Christian scribes who interpreted the words of Jesus in a casuistic manner. Rather his sayings could be interpreted, adapted and applied to new situations. Jesus did not discuss every situation or deal with every problem explicitly, but the tradition of his words can be approached in a living and vital way, precisely because Jesus himself is alive and present with his community (e.g. *Matt.* 28:20). At first sight sayings like Matthew 23:8-10 which declare that there is only one teacher

32. Davies, in *Paul and Rabbinic Judaism,* London 1965, 137-45, discusses the better established parallels from the great epistles.

33. This is the general view in regard to Q, e.g. Harnack, Manson, Dibelius, Taylor. Davies, in *The Setting,* 367-85, considers rather that it deals with the crisis nature of Jesus's preaching of the kingdom, and therefore belongs to kerygmatic rather than catechetical circles.

in the community, Christ, appear strange until we remember the extraordinary awareness of the presence of the risen Christ that the primitive community enjoyed. This helps us to understand why discipleship and its co-relative 'following' can be put forward as the ideal for the Christian community even though they can no longer be carried out literally. The longed-for bringer of final salvation had also acted as teacher in line with his gospel of the kingdom, during his earthly life. Now as the risen and glorified Lord he continues the same function confirming in his new status all that he had said to them while he was still with them (*Matt.* 28:16-20).

Side by side with Paul's use of the words of Jesus, whether implicitly or explicitly, we find that very often he uses the Christian's new life 'in Christ' or their 'life in the Spirit', the idea of a way of life fashioned by the spirit of Christ as a gift received, as the basis for moral argumentation (e.g. 1 *Thess.* 2:10 f.; 5:5 f.; 1 *Cor.* 2:12-16; 6:12-19; *Gal.* 5:1, 16-25; *Rom.* 6; *Col.* 3:1 f.). Indeed some have gone so far as to suggest that this kind of argumentation, imperative based on indicative as it is called, so dominates Paul's ethical thinking that he omits any reference to the earthly life of Jesus.[34] However such a position cannot be maintained. True it is central to his thought, something that the overall structure of his epistles, exhortation following exposition, makes clear. Such a pattern, moral teaching arising from acceptance of Christ and of his Spirit, corresponds to the preaching of Jesus about the kingdom and his moral teaching arising from this. The fact that Jesus preached the kingdom whereas the Church preached the lordship of Jesus points to a terminological, not, however, a substantial, distinction between the two proclamations.[35]

34. See Bultmann, *Theology of the New Testament* (E. tr.), I, London 1955, 188.

35. The object of the 'new quest' for the historical Jesus, is to show the identity between the demands of Jesus's proclamation and those of the early Church. See J. M. Robinson, *A New Quest for the Historical Jesus,* London 1959. In the concluding section (111-25) he describes some

Within such a Christocentric perspective Paul can use both the words of Jesus and commonplace Jewish or even pagan insights into the moral life and place them side by side as instruction for the new life in Christ. Such a juxtaposition of Christian and pagan insights poses no problem for Paul's theology since, as Davies has shown, he presupposes a set of Noachian commandments[36] binding on Jew and Gentile alike, and this accounts for his castigation of both groups for their moral laxity in Romans 1 : 18 – 3 : 20. God's revealed will is universal and binding on all men, something such prophets as Isaiah (2 : 2-4) and Zechariah (8 : 20 f.) had already seen from their reflections on the cosmic lordship of Yahweh.

A good illustration of this combining of the words of Jesus and other moral insights by Paul is to be found in Romans 12-14.[37] 12 : 1-2 introduces moral instruction which is described as 'the will of God' (the Jewish ideal) and 'what is good and pleasing and perfect' (Stoic overtones; cf. *Phil.* 4 : 8). Paul goes on to spell out what this ideal implies by means of specific moral directives. We find here clear echoes of words of Jesus : 12 : 14 (*Matt.* 5 : 44); 12 : 17 (*Matt.* 5 : 39 f.); 12 : 21 (*Matt.* 5 : 38); 13 : 7 (*Matt.* 22 : 15-22); 13 : 8-10 (*Matt.* 22 : 34-40); 14 : 10 (*Matt.* 7 : 1); 14 : 13 (*Matt.* 18 : 7); 14 : 14 (*Matt.* 15 : 11). Fused with this liberal sprinkling of sayings of the master there is other advice which is more in line with the advice of the Stoics : 'do not think of yourself more highly than you ought' (12 : 3); 'live in harmony with one another; do not be haughty, but associate with the lowly' (12 : 16); 'let us conduct ourselves becomingly as in the day' (13 : 13) etc. The whole exposition is given a very definite

---

positive findings with examples of Pauline passages which were clearly influenced by the tradition of Jesus's words. Compare e.g. *Luke* 6 : 20-25 with 1 *Cor.* 4 : 8-13.

36. See *Paul and Rabbinic Judaism*, 112-19. These were a set of commandments which Jewish tradition believed were given to Noah after the flood, and so passed to all men.

37. See C. H. Dodd's treatment of these chapters in *The Epistle to the Romans*, Fontana Books 1959, 198-217.

Christological orientation: 'Put on the Lord Jesus Christ, and make no provision for the flesh to gratify its desires' (13:14). We find a similar use of Greek ethical material in a Christian setting in Galatians.[38] Here Paul takes over lists of vices and virtues current in the Greek world and uses them to describe what is opposed to the 'life in the Spirit' and what are the fruits of the Spirit for the one who is in Christ (*Gal.* 5:1, 2, 6, 16-25).

Attention has often been drawn to the lists of household rules to be found not only in the Pauline epistles but in other New Testament writings as well. Colossians 3:18 – 4:1; Ephesians 5:22 – 6:9 (assuming both to be Pauline); 1 Peter 2:13 f.; Titus 2:1-10; 1 Timothy 2:8 f.; 6:1 f. are the passages usually mentioned in this connection. These lists concern relations between husbands and wives and those between slaves and their masters. The fact that similar instructions are found in both Pauline and non-Pauline letters may possibly indicate a fixed catechism in the early Church dealing with these matters, though probably it was not as well defined as some scholars maintain.[39] When the New Testament versions of these lists are compared with similar Jewish and Hellenistic ones some case could be made for the claim that the Christian lists have a more developed sense of reciprocal responsibility in relations between husbands and wives. However with the possible exception of the Pastorals, the really distinctive element is that the instructions are introduced with a reminder of the Christian's life in Christ (*Col.* 3:18), or as an invitation to follow his example of self-sacrificing love (*Eph.* 5:25; 1 *Pet.* 2:21).

The possible exception in regard to the Pastorals just mentioned prompts us to look more closely at the moral teaching in these letters. There is a definite shift in emphasis here, for the ideal that is placed before the believer in these letters is couched almost entirely in terms from the Greek ethical teaching. For

38. See L. Cerfaux, *Le Chrétien dans la Théologie Paulienne*, Paris 1962, 424-6.

39. E. G. Selwyn, in *The First Epistle of St Peter*, London 1946, gives a detailed reconstruction of this catechesis.

those who accept the Pauline authorship of these letters this is
an indication of the apostle's final adaptation of his gospel to
his audience after he had left Palestine for the last time. Others
see it as one of several internal arguments against the Pauline
authorship.[40] At all events the Greek colouring in the thought
and expression is quite pronounced and it is this that is our chief
concern. The Christian is to live 'soberly, piously and justly in
this life' (*Tit.* 2:12). These were the virtues by which a Stoic
regulated his life with himself, God and his fellow man. All the
virtues that were held in high regard by such philosophers as
Plato, Epictetus, Plutarch are presented in these epistles as the
Christian ideal: truth, goodness, godliness, justice, tranquillity
etc. Even more striking, in the opinion of some, is the absence
of any motivation from Christ's sufferings and death as in the
great epistles. However, we should not overstress this point in
regard to the moral teaching of the Pastorals. In the exhortation
cited above from Titus there is a reminder that they are awaiting
the appearance of our great God and Saviour, Jesus Christ
(cf. also 1 *Tim.* 6:14; 2 *Tim.* 4:1, 8). The epistles are addressed
to those who are 'called by God' (2 *Tim.* 1:9), who can also
be called 'the saints' (1 *Tim.* 5:10). The Christian who is
purified and ready for any good work is like a consecrated vessel
(2 *Tim.* 2:21), in other words, grace and man's will are both
involved in living the Christian life.

We must conclude our survey at this point. In the Christian
communities no less than in the Old Testament there is need for
the people of faith to formulate their own specific moral directives in the light of the new life in Christ that they considered
themselves called on to live. Jesus did not leave a specific code
of morality, but rather the example of his own person. His
words had a very special authority, but they could scarcely be
said to have taken on the character of law, at least not in the
way we normally use that term. Other sources of practical
moral guidance could also be used to describe a Christian way

40. For a detailed discussion of the whole question see C. Spicq, *Les
Épitres Pastorales*, Paris 1947, Introduction, especially cxci-cxcix.

of behaviour in a world that had been originally created in Christ, and was now redeemed by him as his own possession (*Col.* 1 : 16-20).

II. Moral Motivation in the Bible

Our rather lengthy examination of the sources of the Bible's moral teaching has already to some degree answered the second question we posed at the outset, namely, how does biblical morality propose itself to the man of faith? We have seen that in both Old and New Testament alike there is a constant search for a deeper understanding of Yahweh's will and its specific content in relation to the varied circumstances of history and environment in which the people of faith finds itself. In this search help can be had from purely human sources, even if sometimes faith will have a purifying influence on the insights of the 'secular' source. Such a process, undefined and subconscious as it often is, means that Israel is always engaged in relating behaviour to faith. Therefore, her moral teaching can never be arbitrary or imposed, without reference to the faith that motivates man to respond to a God, known in faith. This point is well illustrated by the fact that much of the Bible's moral teaching is set in the context of exhortation: Deuteronomy, the prophets, Jesus, Paul. It could never be mistaken as a cold impersonal law alien to the heart of man. The biblical writers believe that the morality they propose to man is based on the very nature of man 'made in the image of God', and their main preoccupation is to get man, floundering amid all the confusion and obscurity of life, to see where true happiness lies. Repentance, in the sense of returning to one's source, is the very heart of the Bible's moral instruction. Man is exhorted to respond from his own heart rather than imposed upon by legal promulgation.

To this general consideration we may add others in the same line. Firstly, biblical morality is always set in the context of grace. This means that the question of Israel's failure to respond to her God is never seriously considered in the classical periods of her faith. The covenant law comes from the covenant God, as an expression of his love and care for his people. His very name assures Israel of his constant presence with her in each generation (*Exod.* 3:13-15). She is repeatedly reminded that he is the God who brought her out of Egypt, and it is as such that he makes his demands on her. The historical prologue which is part of the classical covenant form serves in the Bible to remind Israel of his gracious acts of kindness in the past (*hesed*), and his loyalty to his pledges in the present (*'emeth*). Thus, e.g. the Decalogue is introduced at Exodus 20:2 with the reminder: 'I am the Lord *your* God, who brought you out of the land of Egypt, out of the house of bondage'. Writing about the Deuteronomic reform, von Rad remarks that there was never any question of Israel not being able to fulfil all the demands; rather, the problem was whether or not Israel was prepared to submit herself to them.[41]

> The law that I enjoin on you today is not beyond your strength or beyond your reach. It is not in heaven, so that you need to wonder, 'Who will go up to heaven for us and bring it down to us so that we may hear it and keep it?' ... No, the word is very near to you, it is in your mouth and in your heart for your observance (*Deut.* 30:11-14).

To say that biblical morality is always set in the context of grace means that good moral living is seen as a response that is drawn from man, and what it should consist in is indicated to man, by the way God acts towards him. The spirit of legalism, on the contrary, is one which sees the imposed code of precepts as measuring exactly how much is demanded of man.

The legalism of the later Jewish period erred not by asking too much from God's people, but by asking too little, and this led to self-sufficiency and a pride that ignored the need for God. Strangely enough this trend towards legalism was started indirectly by those two great prophets of the new covenant, Jeremiah

41. See *Old Testament Theology*, I, 199 f.

and Ezekiel. Faced with interpreting Israel's repeated failures and the calamity of the Babylonian captivity (587 B.C.) so soon after the Deuteronomic reform (622 B.C.), they looked forward to a future covenant that would not be like the old one, for it would be written within the hearts of men and not on tables of stone (*Jer.* 31:31 f.; *Ezek.* 36:24 f.). This criticism of the old law should not be misinterpreted, however. What was really lacking in Israel was the realization that she was in constant need of her saving God. Thorough though the reform of Josiah set out to be, it never achieved this change of heart. The longing of the prophets for a decisive intervention by Yahweh that would bring about such a conversion was fulfilled with the coming of Jesus. As we have seen, his morality is set in the context of God's kingdom as gift (see e.g. the parables of the wicked husbandmen and the king who made the feast for his son, *Matt.* 21:33 – 22:10). The New Testament theologians also recognize this intimate link between grace and morality and develop it fully on the personal and community levels. Side by side with the new commandment of love in John we find the admonition to 'abide in my love' and the promises of the indwelling of the Father and Son and the gift of the Spirit (*John* 13:33 f.; 14:15 f.; 15:5-10). Paul combines the images of Jeremiah and Ezekiel to assure the Christian that the *law* (*Jer.*) of the *Spirit* of life (*Ezek.*) has set them free, and then develops the idea in terms of the indwelling Spirit and the charity that has been poured forth in their hearts (*Rom.* 8:2-11).[42] This is in line with what we have already seen of imperative based on indicative all through his writings. The Christian has put on Christ in baptism, and yet he must be exhorted to put on Christ by a life modelled on that of Christ (*Gal.* 3:27; *Rom.* 13:14).

This leads on to the idea of morality as imitation of God. 'You shall be holy; for I the Lord your God am holy' (*Lev.* 19:2), 'You therefore must be perfect, as your heavenly Father is perfect' (*Matt.* 5:48) and 'Beloved let us love one another . . .

---

42. See S. Lyonnet, Rom. 8:2-4 à la lumière de Jérémie 31 et d'Ézéchiel 35-39', in *Mélanges Eugène Tisserant*, I, Rome 1964, 311-23.

He who does not love does not know God; For God is love'
(1 *John* 4:7 f.) are statements which span the whole biblical
teaching on morality, and they all insist on the divinizing power
found in behaviour that is based on God's own example. The
believer is drawn into union with God not through any form of
mystical experience or secret knowledge, but by conforming his
will to the God who made him. It was the prophets who first
clearly focused attention on morality as central to the God-man
relationship in Israel. In doing so they appealed to man, for
they clearly saw that Yahweh was no patronising divinity in
showing kindness to Israel. Rather election meant that Yahweh
wanted Israel to make herself into what she really was, a holy
people. In the deepest sense possible she could be the maker of
her own destiny; he was helping her and mankind as a whole to
become their true selves. Motivation was not a matter of imposition, of promulgated precepts, but exhortation to respond to
favour and be guided by example.

Old Testament as Torâh

From these general considerations we can examine briefly
some specific points which illustrate how keenly the Bible is
aware of the need to speak to the heart of man. In the first place
it should be noted that the English 'law' corresponds to the
Greek idea of *nomos* as 'custom', 'set rule' or 'standard', but
it does not do full justice to the Hebrew *tôrah*, which literally
means instruction or guidance.[43] That Israel could call the
whole first part of the Bible *tôrah*, shows how she regarded the
details of the law as a gift from Yahweh to help her to fulfil
her covenant commitment. This is further borne out by the fact
that the Decalogue is introduced as the 'words' of Yahweh
(*Exod.* 20:1), and Israel pledging herself to the covenant *tôrah*
can be described as the listening people or the obeying people
since the same Hebrew word *šāma'* covered both ideas (*Exod.*
24:7).

The book of Deuteronomy is perhaps the best example of

43. See C. H. Dodd, *The Bible and the Greeks,* London 1935, 25-41.

tôrah in the Old Testament. The actual Deuteronomic code (chs. 12-26) is introduced by two lengthy addresses put on the lips of Moses. These have a very distinctive tone of exhortation and motivation. The detailed prescriptions of the code have to be read in the light of these speeches which give us the author's viewpoint in regard to law and its function within Israel. In the first place it speaks to the heart of man and it is from the heart that Deuteronomy expects man to respond: 6:4-6; 8:2, 5; 11:13, 18; 26:16; 30:11-20. Besides, the setting is clearly cultic, and each generation is confronted anew with Yahweh's command, giving an existential quality to the preaching. 'Today' becomes a key-word, for in and through the cult Israel is confronted with Yahweh's saving action (*Deut.* 5:3; 9:1-3; 29:2-9), and on the basis of this love a decision is called for from each generation (*Deut.* 30:15-20; cf. 7:12; 8:19; 11:13-16).

Secondly, all the commandments are in fact one commandment, in line with the theme of unity that runs through the book at various levels. This can be seen from the way in which singular and plural, commandment-commandments (*entolē-entolai*), can be used interchangeably at various points throughout the work (*Deut.* 6:24, 25, Hebrew text; 30:10, 11).[44] All the various commandments usually described by the triple formula 'laws, statutes and ordinances', can be summed up in the one commandment of love of God, and as such are the expression of the one will of God for his people. They can equally well be described as God's word (30:11-14), thereby emphasizing the revelational character of the commandments in question. The phrase 'walking in the ways of Yahweh' which is found repeatedly (8:6; 10:12; 11:22; 19:9; 26:17; 28:9; 30:16) to describe man's observance of the statutes, underlines this same insight into the nature of the laws, as revealing the heart and mind of Yahweh as Israel has experienced him in her history.[45]

44 See N. Lohfink, *Höre Ishael, Eine Auslegung von Texten aus dem Buch Deuteronomium*, Die Welt der Bibel 18, Düsseldorf 1965, 61 f

45. See M. J. O'Connell, 'The Concept of Commandment in the Old Testament', *Theological Studies* (21) 1960, 351-403, especially 379-89.

Thus, if they are to be gracious and forgiving to slaves, sojourners and orphans, it is because by doing so they are imitating Yahweh who had acted graciously to Israel amid the slavery of Egypt (10:17-19; 15:12-16; 24:17-18). Yahweh commands in accordance with his own nature.

This overall emphasis of Deuteronomy as 'preached law', to use von Rad's phrase, can be seen in the motivation that within the Deuteronomic code itself is introduced into older statutes previously lacking this.[46] In 14:22, for example, we find an old law about giving a tithe of one's produce to Yahweh, but verses 23-27 is a treatment in homiletic style, explaining now how it may be carried out in the spirit of the present reform. In the later Holiness code of Leviticus 16-26 the same pattern of instruction based on older laws emerges also: at Leviticus 19:17 there is the older negative law: 'You shall not hate your brother in your heart'; to this has now been added a positive instruction: 'But you shall reason with your neighbour lest you bear sin because of him'. Elsewhere in Leviticus we find a similar treatment. Chapter 18 has a structure like that of Deuteronomy. Verses 2-5 give a general instruction to keep the commandments; this is followed by a general commandment (v. 6) which is applied to detailed instances in verses 7-23; the whole is rounded out with a further general exhortation in verses 24-30. It would call for a more detailed study than is possible here to show the changing motivation that was given to various laws throughout the centuries, but for our purposes it is sufficient to show that it was a continual process even within the Decalogue. (Compare *Exod.* 20:8-11 with *Deut.* 5:12-15 on the motivation for the observance of the Sabbath.) In the earliest period it is probable that the mere statement 'I am Yahweh' was sufficient authentication (e.g. the cultic formula in *Lev.* 19). Later a reference to the saving history was a favourite form of such general motivation, as in Exodus 23:15. In the Deuteronomic and Holiness codes we have been examining the fact that individual com-

46. See G. von Rad, *Studies in Deuteronomy*, London 1953, 15-21.

mands were given separate motivation showing that a growing need was felt to awaken in individual Israelites a sense of obligation to their duties, flowing from their covenant faith. The highest form of motive behind the exhortations is the love of God.

Motivation in the Wisdom Literature

Leaving the Pentateuchal material, then, I should like to turn next to the Wisdom literature once again. The first step in the acceptance of the Wisdom material into Israel's religious tradition was taken with the recognition by Isaiah that Yahweh alone was wise (*Is.* 31:1 f.). The next step is the personification of Wisdom, a feature of almost all the canonical Wisdom books (*Prov.* 8:22-36; *Job* 28; *Wis.* 7:22-30; *Sir.* 24; *Bar.* 3:37 – 4:1). It is important to recognize the function of this personification within the Wisdom writings.[47] It is to present the instructions of wisdom in the most attractive and personal form possible; Wisdom personified is the source of life and nourishment for men; she prepares a banquet for them and invites them to her table.[48] Of particular importance is the fact that she has divine origins, and in Job Yahweh himself is thought of as searching for her, and it was he alone who discovered her.

Wisdom was present with Yahweh at the creation of the world, and consequently she knows the secrets of the world, and the ways of God and men. By accepting her instruction and guidance man can share in these secrets and partake in the divine life that she enjoys with Yahweh. The exact scope of Wisdom's understanding varies from writer to writer. In Proverbs and Job she understands the creation, and so she can share with men the mysteries of life and death. In Sirach and Baruch she is identified with the law, and therefore she represents Yahweh's special gift to Israel. This development is in line with the conservative

47. See R. N. Whybray, *Wisdom in Proverbs,* London 1965, 90-104.

48. Many exegetes see a similar pattern in Christ's invitation to his disciples to come to him, *Matt.* 11:25-29; *Luke* 10:21-22; see A. Feuillet, 'Jésus et la Sagesse divine d'après les Évangiles Synoptiques', *Revue Biblique* (52) 1955, 161-96.

tendencies of late Judaism in Palestine, but as yet such extolling of the law has not fallen into legalism. The author delights in the law (cf. *Ps.* 119), and there is no question about Israel's inability to fulfil it. Rather it is her special privilege to possess such a precious gift from Yahweh. By contrast the Hellenistic book of Wisdom sees her as possessing the knowledge of all the sciences, medicine, astrology, science etc., so highly culti- vated in Alexandria. It is clear then that the personification of Wisdom and the dignity she possesses because of her divine origin are intended by the Wisdom writers to make her and her teaching acceptable to a people who had long been taught to mistrust such maxims as coming from the enemy of Yahweh.

New Testament Morality, a Morality of Love

Finally we turn to the Johannine writings, for in our survey of the New Testament literature in the first part of this essay we did not mention these, precisely because they seem to have little interest in the specific moral teaching of Jesus. The emphasis is centred on the love commandment as the one concrete ethical instruction of Jesus for his disciples. It is called a 'new' com- mand, presumably because it is revealed in and through the ministry of Jesus in a new way. By contrast with the Synoptics it is only love of the brother that is mentioned: John 3:34; 15:12; 1 John 2:8-10; 3:11; 4:7-12. 1 John 4:21 is the one excep- tion, for it also mentions a command to love God, explaining at the same time that this is an empty formula unless one loves the brother whom one sees as a proof of the genuineness of the desire to love.

In discussing this concentration of John on the command to love the brother there are two aspects of his work as a whole that must be kept in mind. In the first place we find a fluctuation between command and commandments, just as in Deuteronomy, and this should put us on our guard against understanding John as having no interest in specific moral directives of Jesus.[49]

49. See R. Brown, *The Gospel according to John, I-XII*, Anchor Bible 29, New York 1966, Appendix 1 (5) *entolē*, 504 f.

The disciples are told about a new commandment (*entolē*, sing.) at 13:34 and 15:12, whereas at 14:15, 21 they are told to keep his commandments (*entolai*, plur.). Furthermore, the Spirit is promised explicitly to the disciples to remind them of all that Jesus had said to them (*John* 14:26), and to lead them into all truth (16:12-14). John is far from ignoring the specific words of Jesus but he wants them to be understood in their deepest significance and to integrate them into a higher synthesis.[50]

This gives a clue to the second aspect of John's theology that is of supreme importance for his moral teaching, and again Deuteronomy is a useful background for understanding his thought. We saw how in the Old Testament book the commands given have a revelational aspect, they are the word of God to his community (*Deut.* 30:11-14). The central emphasis of John is, as is well known, the revelation that Jesus, as the Word who was with God, brings into the world (*John* 1:1-4). He has come to bear witness to the truth (*John* 18:37), because he is the truth, in fact the way and the life as well (*John* 14:6). His earthly life has been one of complete obedience to the Father's will (*John* 4:34; 5:30; 6:38), that is a carrying out of the command he received from his Father (10:18 *entolē*, sing.) or a keeping of the Father's commandments, thereby abiding in his love (*John* 15:10 *entolai*, plur.). In other words his life is a model or exemplar of what he is now asking of his disciples. His life of love was a revelation of the God of love (1 *John* 4:7-12), and the new command is to love one another, *as he has loved us* (*John* 15:12 f.). 'By this we *know* love that he laid down his life for us; and we ought to lay down our lives for the brethren' (1 *John* 3:16). In other words, Christ's life of love in obedience to the command he received from his Father reveals to us the kind of life we must lead. Our eyes are turned firmly towards the 'life that was made manifest among us' (1 *John*

50. See N. Lazure, *Les Valeurs Morales de la Théologie Johannique,* Paris 1965 (Études Bibliques), 123-58.

1 : 2), that is, towards the Word that became flesh in our midst
(*John* 1 : 14), to discover the pattern our own lives must follow.

In Deuteronomy the Israelites were exhorted to 'walk in the
ways of Yahweh', that is to reproduce Yahweh's attitude by
imitating him in their dealings with their fellow men. In doing
so they became like Yahweh. In John God has come nearer to
man in Christ, the Word made flesh, and we are now to imitate
him. We must follow him, that is be his disciples, because he
has shown us in a unique way 'how to walk in the ways of
Yahweh', in selfless giving of himself for others. It is thus that
man can attain to the great Other that is God, and this is his
greatest privilege and dignity. It is because John wished to con-
centrate on this supreme motivation for Christian behaviour
that he has focused all the attention on the command to love the
brother, to the apparent neglect of the other specific moral directives of Jesus. This one command summarizes perfectly the
whole life of him who is the way, the truth and the life.

Conclusion

This enquiry into biblical morality has revealed a number of
constants in both Old and New Testament, which answer our
questions posed at the beginning. In the first place faith and
revelation never dispense God's people from the task of discovering the pattern their behaviour should take in changing historical circumstances. The starting point for this search is always
their faith-experience of God, the God of the exodus in the Old
Testament, and the God who was in Christ, reconciling the world
to himself, in the New. Convinced that their behaviour must
always reflect this God who had revealed himself in and through
his dealings with them in their history, they may use the contemporary insights into the good life with which they come in
contact, refining them where necessary in line with the particular
stage of their awareness of God and their current understanding
of his nature. The actual content of their morality will thus be
often similar to that of their surrounding neighbours, at least in
the more lofty formulations of these, but there is now the added

assurance that what they are doing is God's will for them, and at the same time the appreciation that by acting in this way, man is attaining to his true self, which is to be like God.

On the other hand, we must never ignore the fact that this very assurance carried with it real dangers for Israel's moral teaching. The example we cited from early Israel, where her less sophisticated way of life meant that she had not formulated the rights of women as clearly or explicitly as had her urbanized neighbours, points to a danger that the very vividness of the awareness that moral behaviour was the fulfilment of Yahweh's will for his people could cause indifference to exploring all the possible areas of man's response and failure. It has been suggested by Eichrodt that the relatively few casuistic laws in the Book of the Covenant by comparison with the Code of Hammurabi shows how Israel was prepared to leave many areas to the individual's personal responsibility.[51] This suggestion is, however, open to question. An alternative conclusion would be that early Israel, so deeply conscious of its corporate nature, tended to overlook individual obligations. A case could be made for saying that because she was so keenly aware of her unity before Yahweh as one person, her early laws covered only those areas of moral conduct in which the community harmony and unity was likely to be disrupted. It was only with the breakdown of this corporate moral responsibility in the exilic period (see e.g. *Ezek.* 18) that areas of individual rights and duties as such were explored in any depth.

Certainly, the casuistry and legalism of the later period with its multiplicity of particular precepts had the effect of deadening any sense of response to a loving God. It was this corrosion of the religiously motivated response from the heart that called forth such vigorous condemnation from Jesus. Useful though the covenant idea was for expressing the all-embracing character of Israel's relationship with Yahweh, there was always inherent in it certain dangers for a correct understanding of the true

51. *Theology of the Old Testament*, I, 77.

nature of that relationship. A covenant of grace and love (*Hos.* 11:1-9) easily became one of contract (*Sir.* 44:20 f.), and once this misplacing of emphasis had taken place, the transition from a response in love to one of formalism and externalism followed inevitably. This danger was not obviated with the advent of the new covenant in Christ, as the bitter judaizing controversy in the early Church shows clearly. Paul's epistle to the Galatians is a vigorous defence of Christian liberty by the apostle, liberty, that is, to serve freely by walking in the Spirit. The law coming much later can never annul the promise made to Abraham, and Christians as children of Abraham, must never allow the personal faith-response to Christ, inaugurated at baptism, to degenerate into a set of practices and observances, however laudable in themselves. Matthew, by building Christ's words into a Messianic torah in the Sermon on the Mount (*Matt.* 5:17-20) may well have obscured somewhat the real originality of Christ as moral teacher. Behind each of the special instructions of the Sermon, stands the kingdom as proclaimed by Jesus, that is, God's self-giving gift to man and his invitation to man to live out this gift in his life, after the model of Jesus's own life. Unless this fact is kept firmly at the centre there is a real danger of reducing the moral teaching of Jesus to a code of morality, a neo-Pharisaism purged of the more extreme elements, but still emphasizing details rather than attitude, the letter rather than the spirit. It would be interesting in the light of this, to trace the extent to which the undoubted popularity of the first gospel in the Church has influenced the subsequent approach to Christian morality.

In the last analysis it is this emphasis on the spirit that is the distinctive and original contribution of the Bible to moral thinking. If a member of the people of faith is given the assurance of having the divine goodness as the proper context for his moral behaviour, he is also challenged by that goodness to make a free personal choice and a consequent re-orientation of his life. The self-disclosure of God as the people of faith experienced it, was in terms of love, whether covenant love in the Old Testament, or the incarnate love of the historical Jesus in the New.

The intensity and the personal quality of the experience is new with the coming of Christ (*kainos*), that is, of a different order, but it still retains the essential quality of love. God's love has been concretized and humanized in Christ, and it is from him that we must learn the demands on self that genuine love makes. His freedom from self that characterized his life unto death, and his care and concern for human misery in all its forms, even the slavery of the self-opinionated teachers to their own systems, were the features of his life as he was remembered (*John* 2:22; 12:16). It was this that constituted the basis for his radical call to men to follow him. The Church was keenly aware of the need to retain such a picture of the historical Jesus, with the authority of his truth, wholeness and sincerity, side by side with 'theological' motivation arising from life 'in Christ', as can be seen from the fact that Paul's epistle to the Romans and Mark's gospel were written to the same Roman Church within the space of a few years. This does not mean that Jesus's life and sayings were considered normative in any literalist way, as we have seen. Rather, this gospel record is valid and necessary as showing how within his particular spiritual history God's demand could be lived out to the full, and 'crowned with honour and glory'. It is this that constitutes at once the uniqueness and absoluteness of Christ, and his attractiveness to draw men to imitate his selflessness when faced with the supreme demand of God. The gospel accounts are not merely a record of the past success of Jesus's own historical living out of the demands of the kingdom; they are *anamnēsis*, or representation, witnessing to the possibilities of achieving similar success in their own lives, that Jesus, as glorified Lord, is offering to men in the present.

All this would seem to have very important consequences for the Church as teacher of morals. Her consciousness of herself as bearer of revelation should never cause her to ignore the world and its moral standards or systems of behaviour. Aware of the fact that the people of faith, as reflected in the Bible, discovered much of the content of its moral teaching from 'the world', the Church must never consider herself as a last bulwark

against a permissive society, however accurate such general-
izations may appear to be at any given time. The exchange with
the world in the matter of morality will be much more fruitful
for the Church and the world if she realizes that she can on
occasion learn from it. Provided she is prepared to observe and
listen, she may discover areas, particularly so-called 'human'
areas, in which the world has outstripped her in the sharpness of
its discovery and formulation of man's dignity and his consequent rights and duties.

Furthermore, the teaching Church must always remember that
morality in the Christian context is man's response from the
heart. Accordingly, she must as teacher propose rather than
impose. She must never hesitate to present the radical demands
of Christ, but this must be done in such a way that the ideal in
question is seen as the ideal of Christ, and the radicality of the
demand, his radicalness. She will recognize that like Jesus her
moral teaching must flow from the gospel she preaches, and be
based on her own living commitment to that gospel. Here lies
her greatest privilege, but also her most urgent challenge as
teacher of Christian morals. In particular, she must never suc-
cumb to the all too human temptation to become patronising
and protective of man because of his failures and sinfulness, by
turning the demand of God into a largely negative and over-
elaborate legal system that asks too little of the individual's
responsibility. In that event she would be doing less than justice
to God's gift and man's faith. In particular she would be
obscuring the fact that Christ's most radical demand was made
within the context of repentance and forgiveness, and that the
gospel of the kingdom was a message of continuing love and
salvation in the present, without the threat of immediate apoc-
alyptic judgement for failures, something his contemporaries,
even John the Baptist, could not fully appreciate or understand
(*Matt.* 3:4-12; 11:2-6).

PAGAN PHILOSOPHY AND CHRISTIAN ETHICS

'God has not been so sparing to men, to make them barely
two-legged creatures and left it to Aristotle to make them
rational.' Nor, what Locke did not need to add, to make them
moral. Nor for that matter, we may add, did God leave it to
Christianity. One could scarcely remain Christian and maintain
that Christianity was unimportant for morals. But even the most
enthusiastic Christian could scarcely assert that there were no
moral men before Christianity. It is not the purpose of this
chapter to establish what, if anything, was absolutely new in the
content of Christian moral teaching. And, on the other hand, it
would be naïve even to think of tracing a possible relation of
dependence between Christian and pagan moral teaching just
because Aristotle, for example, held that adultery, theft and
murder were wrong in all circumstances. What I am attempting
rather is to indicate ways of thinking and sometimes, too, concepts and phrases which proved important in the expression of
Christian moral teaching. They are not all indicated, nor are the
philosophical asserted to be the only influences on Christian
moral teaching. The Jewish legalistic tradition is at least as important as anything I shall mention. But I would like to draw
attention to early expositions by some key figures of three related
ideas which recur throughout the history of Christian morals.

39

These are, firstly, a seductive concept of truth, secondly, the description of Christ as the *Logos*, and thirdly, the natural law tradition.

St Augustine writes in the *Confessions*: 'Further, I read there, in the Platonists, that your only-begotten Son was before all times and beyond all times and abides unchangeably, co-eternal with you, and that of his fullness souls receive, that they may be blessed, and that by participation in that wisdom which abides in itself they are renewed that they may be wise' (7, 14). The passage and its context is revealing for the attitude of the early Christian intellectuals of whom Augustine is in this instance typical. The fact that a Christian teaching could be found paralelled in a pagan philosopher added greatly to its suasory value. The parallel was taken to reflect credit on both Christianity and pagan philosophy. The best philosophy was evidently a foreshadowing of Christianity which God in his wisdom had granted to the heathens: and Christianity was glad to adopt and improve the formulations which were current among the educated pagans of the day. In that way Christianity became intellectually respectable. It combined two styles of language and seemed to fuse perfectly two bodies of truth. As Justin said: 'Christ is the Logos, in whom the whole human race has a portion, and all who have lived according to this Logos are Christians, even though, like Socrates and Heraclitus among the Greeks, they are accounted godless' (*Apologia*, 1, 46).

The philosophical influence on the growing Church came from two main sources, Platonism and Stoicism. For Christian ethics attention has been concentrated, and perhaps rightly, on the Stoic influence. But before turning to it, it is important to remark on a feature of Platonism which was potentially more important, because more radical, for Christian ethics. This was the Platonic concept of truth.

Many early Christians found Platonism attractive. It provided a theory for the type of Christianity which thought only of fleeing the world: its 'two-world' structure was ideally suited to this sort of thought. Its transcendence left man and his world in a position which was as low as even the most fervid supporters of original sin could dream out. At the same time it was extremely intellectualist and believed firmly in the importance of having this imperfect world conformed to the reliable standards which did exist and which the philosophers, who would if possible be kings, were familiar with and had a duty to apply. The Platonic approach to the truth was a mathematical method which would make all genuine knowledge depend on an intuitional grasp of the Good. The philosopher knew the truth through his acquaintance with the Good. He would try to improve his city by the formulation of laws: 'Laws would seem to be written copies of scientific truth in the various departments of life they cover, copies based as far as possible on the instructions received from those who really possess the scientific truth on these matters' (*Statesman*, 300c). The human city should be governed as far as possible by divine laws.

Much ink has been spilt, particularly in the last thirty years, in pointing out the dangers inherent in Plato's paternalistic attitude to political morality. It would not have been so attacked by some had it not been so attractive to others. Augustine thought that of all the pagans the Platonists had come nearest to Christianity: 'No school has come closer to us than the Platonists' (*Civ. Dei* 8, 5). And from a time long before the writing of *The City of God*, from the earliest works written after his conversion, we can see what was for him the attraction of the Platonic approach to the truth. He hungers for the truth that is unchanging, like the truth of mathematics: this immortal truth should be our goal, 'to see God, the fountain from which issues all truth, the very father of truth' (*De Ord.* II, 51). This, he thought, had been the secret of Plato 'the wisest and most learned man of his day'. Plato had realized that 'there are two worlds, the intelligible world, where truth itself dwells, and the sensible', which we can see and touch. And of these, the first is 'itself true, the second is like truth and made in its image' (*C. Acad.* 3, 37).

Augustine was, therefore, inclined to picture the mind as having in the intelligible world intelligible objects just as in the sensible world there are sense-objects. 'We must not say that the things which you and I both perceive mentally belong to the nature of our minds. For what the eyes of two persons see simultaneously cannot be identified with something belonging to the eyes of either one or the other, but must be some third thing to which the sight of both is directed' (*De Lib. Arb.* 2, 33). 'Reason is the mind's sight whereby it perceives truth through itself, without the intermediary of the body' (*De Immort. An.* 10).

Augustine was helped towards this extreme position on truth by the inclination to scepticism which he found in himself. It is significant that the first work he wrote after turning to Christianity was against the sceptical Academy. His first need was to convince himself. He maintained that some truths cannot be doubted: these are the propositions of logic and mathematics and basic certainties of moral judgement. There was a natural tendency to expand this area of certainty: a definition of 'wisdom' which he likes to repeat is 'the knowledge of all things, human and divine'. The intelligible world is from another viewpoint the divine mind which contains the ideas of all created things. The intellectual light which renders these forms intelligible is a divine illumination within the human mind which provides it with rules for judgement. Our actions and judgements about them are measured against the absolute standard of human conduct seen in the light of divine illumination.[1] 'In this eternal truth, which is the origin of all temporal things, we behold by a perception of the mind (*visu mentis*) the pattern which governs our being and activities, whether in ourselves or in regard to other things, according to the rule of truth and right reason' (*De Trin.* 9, 12).

The point could, of course, be made that if this Platonic theory of truth had not existed the Church would have invented it. For even if naïve it is natural and, for an idealist, seductive. There would seem to be little point in looking for the truth if one does not look for the whole truth. Since it did exist it was

1. See R. Markus, 'Augustine', in *A Critical History of Western Philosophy* (ed. D. J. O'Connor), New York 1964, 89.

natural that a Churchman like Augustine should adopt it. The fact that a pagan had come to it by his own efforts would re-assure a Christian bishop who knew that in the meantime God had imparted this truth even more clearly through Christ. He would seem a very half-hearted Christian who, when asked whether we had in Christ the full truth, hesitated to give his assent. And if a philosopher would try to provide laws as perfect as possible for an ordinary earthly city, it was very little to expect a Christian to work out laws for the city of God. Any efforts that Augustine made were taken up enthusiastically by the men who followed him. For his reputation and influence were immense. His admirers and supporters range from Pope Celestine just after his death up to and beyond the Jansenists: the thirtieth proposition as condemned by Alexander XII in 1690 runs: 'Whatever doctrine one finds clearly rooted in Augustine can be held and taught without regard for any Apostolic Bull'.

Stoicism was, as remarked above, the other main philosophic influence on Christianity. This is, at first sight, strange, for the first Stoics were strict materialists and Augustine himself is on occasion scornful of their views. But their language, in fact, often did not measure up to the strict demands of their theory (Cleanthes' Hymn to Zeus is a good example of the contrast), and they had provided Christianity with many useful terms in the expression of some of its central dogmas. One of their distinctions seemed ready-made for Christianization: this was the distinction between *logos endiathetos* and *logos proforikos,* the internal word or thought and the word as uttered. The word as uttered was the Word that came out from God the Father. This Word was Christ. The distinction between *logos endiathetos* and *logos proforikos,* then, seemed a very useful one in the earliest Christian speculation about the Trinity and was eagerly pursued. In course of time, however, it was seen to have its own difficulties, and eventually it was thought necessary, at the Synod of Sirmio in 351, to ban the use of the distinction when speaking of the Son of God who came out from the Father.

The banning of this distinction did not, of course, entail the removal of the term Logos from Christian thought. The speculation about the Logos up to that time, in Theophilus, Tertullian, Tatian, Justin, Irenaeus, Origen and Clement, had ensured that the term would have a long history in theology. But this speculation in itself was, obviously, only of secondary importance: what really counted was the fact that the term Logos had been applied to Christ in the prologue to the gospel of St John. 'In the beginning was the Logos, and the Logos was with God, and the Logos was God.' Why John used Logos does not interest us here. It has been suggested that he was influenced by the example of the Wisdom literature of the Old Testament, and that, like Philo of Alexandria, he wanted to bring together the Greek-Stoic and the Jewish traditions. The fact is that he did use the term for Christ, and that for many Christians it became a favoured expression, particularly when they wanted to demonstrate the intellectual respectability of Christianity.

Yet the term Logos conceals one of the basic tensions of Christian ethics. Christ was love, and man was to be in love with Christ. But how could one be in love with a word, formula or proposition which were normal meanings of *logos*? Moreover, in the philosophic tradition from which it came, *logos* was the formula or law of the regular order of events. *Logos* was also called Zeus or God, but a transcendent God was not intended (indeed, any sort of spiritual element was specifically ruled out by the Stoics): what was meant was the right reason which pervades all things, separable by the mind but in fact always coexisting with and informing matter, the passive principle. Another name for it is Fate, the determined order of events, the plan of God.

There is no doubt that, given this tradition, the combination of Christ as *Logos* and as Saviour *could* have led to moral absolutism of the most stringent kind. Cicero, talking of the theories of Zeno, the first Stoic, says: 'Zeno's view is that the law of nature (=Logos) is divine, and that its function is to command what is right and forbid the opposite. How he makes out this law to be alive passes our comprehension, yet we undoubtedly expect God to be a living being' (*De Nat. Deorum* 1, 36). The notion of a living law in Christianity could have produced a claim to absolute control over man's words and even thoughts, not to mention his actions. It would have meant the end of all freedom of choice, and therefore of all morality.

It is basically the same difficulty as that which we saw when discussing Augustine's concept of truth. In both cases there is a tendency to combine and interchange two different kinds of knowledge, the knowledge of propositions and knowledge by acquaintance. And some Churchmen were undoubtedly led to believe that because the Church had come to the knowledge of Christ the way, the truth and the life (knowledge by acquaintance), it was therefore in possession of all the truth that can be communicated in propositions about faith or morals. But the practical results of such an attitude are, for various reasons, not so important in the Greek-Alexandrian tradition, where the *Logos* speculation had been concentrated. To see these results we must turn to the Roman tradition and its Latin translation of the Stoic *Logos*, the *lex naturae*.

Cicero, who has just been quoted, was acquainted with a great deal of Greek philosophy and is one of the most important links in its transmission to the Latin world. He belonged to no school, but the Stoic and Platonic philosophies were dominant at his time. (The very sane Aristotelian ethical tradition was in eclipse and remained so for centuries.) Cicero was an advocate and a would-be statesman, and his life dictated his philosophical interests. When he was forced out of politics he turned to translating Greek philosophy which, he felt, could be of use to Rome. He transmitted ideas which would help to guarantee a good system of government in Rome and for the world. One of those ideas was 'the law of nature'.

The term 'law of nature' occurs for the first time in Western

philosophy in the *Gorgias* of Plato: Callicles there uses it to
mean the right of the strong to have his way with the weak. The
ambiguity inherent in the term, springing from the varieties of
meaning of both 'law' and 'nature', could scarcely be made more
obvious. One would have thought that after such a beginning it
would be useless for everything except obscuring issues. But
Aristotle restored it to respectability by showing, in the *Rhetoric*
(1373b), how the law of nature can be appealed to when one
wishes to ignore the narrow prescriptions of particular law-
codes: Antigone's action was a good example of this, he says.
And it was in this sense that the Stoics took it up: that is, to
mean something superior to and corrective of all positive law.
The demand to follow the law of nature meant for man simply
the demand to act morally. 'The law of nature' was simply
another name for morality: it did not, and was not meant to,
add anything to its content. To that extent, it was and is irrelevant to morality. In fact, for *moral* theory it would have been
better if the term had never been used: its chief function there
has been to create confusion by permitting rapid shifting of
ground between meanings of law, as description of observed
regularities or prescription of an approved way of acting, and
meanings of nature as biological order or as ideal human
behaviour. Other disadvantages will be noted later.

Where 'the law of nature' has been useful is in the *legal* sphere,
as providing an ideal to which all positive law-codes should
conform. The service which the Stoic philosophers rendered here
was due partly to the situation in which they found themselves.
Zeno, the first Stoic, is reckoned to have been a few years
younger than Alexander the Great and to have outlived him by
about sixty years. The Greek city-state was replaced by a new
internationalism. Chrysippus, the third head of the school, was
born about 280 B.C. when a successor of Alexander was coming
into contact with a new and expanding power, Rome. The whole
context of their thought forced on them a broad conception of
law: man's responsibilities were not bounded by the particular
state or community in which he lived. Zeno's *Politeia*, appar-

ently, did for the world-state what Plato's *Politeia* had done for the city-state, 'shaping as it were a dream or picture of a philosophic, well-ordered society', where 'we should regard all men as our fellow-countrymen and fellow-citizens ... under a common law' (Plutarch, *De Alex. Magni Fortuna aut Virtute*, 329 a-b). Chrysippus, too, maintained that 'the nature of man is such that a kind of social code exists between the individual and the rest of the human race' (Cicero, *De Finibus* 3, 67).

Living 'according to nature' meant then living as man should live in society. But a fragment from Chrysippus preserved by Diogenes Laertius points to the root of later confusions: 'Living virtuously is equivalent to living in accordance with experience of the actual course of nature, as Chrysippus says in the first book of his *About Ends;* for our individual natures are parts of the actual course of nature', as Chrysippus says in the first may be defined as life in accordance with nature, or in other words, in accordance with our own human nature as well as that of the universe, a life in which we refrain from every action forbidden by the law common to all things, that is to say, the right reason which pervades all things and is identical with this Zeus, lord and ruler of all that is' (*Lives of Eminent Philosophers*, VII, 86-8).

Confusions will arise unless distinctions are made. For in one sense our individual natures are parts of the nature of the whole universe. But it also belongs to the nature of man particularly to interfere with the nature of other things and the nature of the universe. So life in accordance with our human nature takes account of the nature of the rest of the universe but attempts to transcend it. Man too does refrain from actions forbidden by the law common to all things. But some actions are 'forbidden' because they are, permanently or temporarily, physically impossible, whereas man refrains from other actions which are physically possible (and, to that extent, in accordance with nature) because he thinks he should not do them. And, finally, the quotation from Chrysippus suggests a difficulty which goes to the heart of their system. For they held that fate is the same as

Logos or God, God expressing himself in the regular order of events. The problem then is, what scope is really left for the knowledge and activity of man? What point is there in talking of right and wrong if man has no self-direction but is simply part of a process which will take place anyway and which cannot be changed? Does their system really allow for freedom? And can there be morals without freedom? The problem becomes particularly acute when the attempt is made to turn the Stoic theory, which in practice was fairly flexible, into a legal system. And this was the direction of development when Stoicism entered the Roman world. The Roman genius was legal rather than philosophical. And the Roman system in turn influenced canon law. But the original confusion was that of the early Stoics in associating the will of God so closely with a physical process.

There are more specific difficulties for Stoicism as an ethical theory. And if particular moral positions which were attributed to them had been strict deductions from a 'natural law theory', it seems unlikely that natural law morality would have enjoyed the esteem which it later did enjoy in the Church. The Church would not have permitted some of the things which the Stoics are said to have permitted, suicide, for instance (Diog. Laert. VII, 130), nor would it have recommended community of wives for an ideal state (*ibid.*, 131), nor have countenanced incest (*ibid.*, 187), nor homosexuality, nor prostitution (Sextus Empiricus, *P.H.* 3, 198 f.). And if 'the Christians shared with the Stoics, or took from them the assumption that there was a natural law by which acts unworthy of human beings might be judged',[2] we must remember that it is a very flexible standard we have to deal with.

There was, however, relatively little direct contact between these Greek Stoics as revealed in their writings and the vast majority of early Christian writers. The spread of the natural law theory in the Church was due rather to the influence of

---

2. J. T. Noonan, *Contraception: A History of its Treatment by Catholic Theologians and Canonists,* Harvard 1965, 46.

Latin writers like Cicero and Seneca, reinforced at a later date by the prestige of the classical Roman jurists. The influence of Cicero is preponderant in the Latin writers – Lactantius, Ambrose and Augustine are good examples of it. In fact, as Thamin says, Cicero became a Father of the Church himself. Lactantius (*Inst.* 6, 8) could only explain Cicero's words in *Rep.* 3, 33 on the law of nature by supposing that he was inspired. A more obvious and prosaic source for these words is, however, Panaetius (c. 190-109 B.C.) the leader of the Middle Stoa, who took up residence in Rome in the middle of the second century B.C. Not that Panaetius had anything new to add to the teaching of Zeno or Chrysippus on the law of nature: what was significant about him was that he taught in Rome, as did Posidonius who succeeded him. The Romans were men of action, concerned with good government: they were proud of their law, and in their constant efforts to develop it further they fell gratefully on the concept of 'natural law'. It was the standard to which they could appeal when altering rigid laws to meet modern needs.

Cicero was aware of a distinction between law and moral philosophy (*De Off.* 3, 68: 'sed aliter leges, aliter philosophi tollunt astutias, leges quatenus manu tenere possunt, philosophi, quatenus ratione et intellegentia'), but it was not a distinction which he was concerned to define. For, in general, like the Greeks, he wanted to emphasize that ethics and politics are continuous, and he wanted to give to law the universality of morality and to ethics the binding force of law. Consequently he slipped easily into the habit of speaking of the demands of natural morality as if it were a law. Moreover, whatever Cicero's own belief in God may have been, he was aware that the Divinity is an effective rhetorical weapon, and improved this law of nature by calling it not only the human but also the divine law: he spoke of 'ipsa naturae ratio', 'which is the human and divine law, and he who obeys this – and all who wish to live according to nature will obey it – will never be guilty of seeking what is not his own' (*De Off.* 3, 23). It should be emphasized that this was primarily a rhetorical flourish: Cicero did not feel called upon to analyse the term 'ipsa naturae ratio quae est lex divina et humana', or to make the necessary distinctions between the extent of human and divine knowledge and the sort of law which could therefore follow from each. He wished only to indicate God's approval for action in accordance with human nature: at the same time he would scarcely have objected if it was implied that human specifications of that action were also God's direct instructions to man.

It is natural that this confusion of the scope of divine and human knowledge should be increased when natural law specification was taken up by a Church which believed that it already was in possession of a code of moral behaviour sanctioned by Christ the way, the truth and the life. If the Church was in any way superior to the state it was natural to believe that it should have a clearer insight into God's plan, that it should be capable of enunciating this plan for man's moral activity with more precision and finesse, and that it should have the right of demanding from its members a correspondingly higher standard of behaviour.

Such an attitude is apparent in the *De Officiis Ministrorum* of St Ambrose, for instance. And while the theory of the two cities was written by Augustine it was a lived reality for Ambrose whom the people of Milan had forced to become their bishop even though he was not yet baptized and was present only to keep order in his capacity as governor of the province. He did not see the step from governorship to bishopric as demotion: 'We priests have our own ways of rising to Empire. Our infirmity is our way to the throne.' He dealt with the imperial court and his ex-colleagues of the civil authority with the easy assurance of one who has retired at the top to devote himself to higher things. He was, moreover, a highly educated man, conversant with the Alexandrian tradition, treating his congregations on Sundays to sermons incorporating lengthy quotations from Plotinus.

But though Ambrose knew the Greek tradition and, unlike

Augustine, could read it easily in the original, he was by temperament much closer to the Latin. This is obvious in his *De Officiis Ministrorum*, the very title of which is an acknowledgment of his reliance on Cicero. 'Et sicut Tullius ad erudiendum filium, ita ego quoque ad vos informandos filios meos' (1, 24). He too, like Cicero and following him, uses the language of 'imitating nature' (1, 84) and the law of nature, but for Ambrose these phrases evidently mean something other than what they meant for Cicero, not to speak of the Cynic-influenced branch of Stoicism for whom following nature meant 'doing what the animals do'. He does not, however, analyse the modifications which a changed concept of nature entails. An exhortation not to act 'against nature' is an exhortation not to do anything disgraceful or unbecoming (cf. 1, 124 and 222). When man acts 'in accordance with human nature', on the other hand, he stands out from other living things because he looks for the reasons for things and thinks that he must search out the ground of his own being, who rules all things and to whom we must account for all our acts. He says that nothing helps more towards leading a decent life than the belief in this future judge whom nothing escapes, whom good actions please and bad offend (1, 125). It is obvious that a great deal has been added to the original substrata from Cicero-Panaetius, but Ambrose does not feel called on to invoke revelation. What 'natural' reason discovers evidently will not clash with revelation: there is, therefore, no need to pursue the analysis further.

This procedure is typical of Ambrose. In the chapters immediately following (1, 127 f.), for example, he borrows very directly from Cicero's translation of Panaetius on the fundamental virtues, but then points out that the gospel has improved on the philosophers' exposition of the primary function of justice and therefore rendered it null and void. There is more piety than hard thought in this remark, and Ambrose follows it with the assertion that what good there was in Stoic teaching on community relations was borrowed from the Scriptures (1, 132 f.).

Ambrose did not, of course, have to defend these positions in

rigorous philosophical or historical debate. He is not interested
in strict deduction: when he uses the natural law argument to
recommend a particular course of action he is doing nothing
more than asserting a moral order in the universe (v. 1, 228 f.
and 3, 21 f.). When he combines the 'law of nature' with revelation, it is sometimes, as above, to point out the superiority of
the gospel, and sometimes to move easily from one to the other
without signalling any break in the argument: 'violatur natura
generis humani, et sanctae Ecclesiae congregatio' (3, 19). But no
serious effort is made to contrast and evaluate the contributions
of 'nature' or of revelation nor to test the cogency of the arguments derived. This was due partly to the literary form which he
was following, an exhortation to the good life based on wisdom
where a meticulous investigation of the cogency of the different
arguments would have been out of place. In such a treatise it is
better that people should be urged to do too much lest they be
encouraged to do too little.

And although Ambrose's *De Officiis Ministrorum* is the only
systematic ethical treatise in the early Latin Church, as Clement's *Paedagogus* is in the Greek, his attitudes are not unique.
Augustine and Ambrose became two of the four Greater Doctors
of the West. Together they took natural law from Cicero, baptized it and handed it on for preservation in the Church. As
Augustine said, 'The eternal law is the Divine reason or the will
of God which commands that the natural order be preserved
and forbids it to be disturbed' (*Contra Faustum* 22, 7).

But the natural order was not only to be preserved. The idea
that grace perfects nature took root early in the Church and the
perfection took different forms. The Church was the perfect
society, and its laws could be expected to represent an advance
on the laws of ordinary society. The fact that at times the new
law appeared more demanding and oppressive than the old was
taken as a sign of its authenticity. For after the Fall the law of
nature would obviously become evident in the form of an order
of compulsion. The law of nature in our state must be a remedy
for sin. Even that notion itself was a 'perfection' of a theme to

be found in Cicero and Seneca: they too saw in submission to ordered government a remedy against wickedness. The tradition of a golden age in the past is a strong one in Greek and Latin literature: the age in which men now lived was one of sad decline. The Fathers, then, could readily understand the idea of harshness as a punishment for sin. And this was made palatable in a more positive way by the adoption of the Stoic doctrine that the blessedness of the life of virtue is independent of external circumstance. Ambrose maintains, 'A blessed life does not depend on external advantages, but on virtue only' (*De Off.* 2, 18). Consequently, 'the wise man is not broken by bodily pains nor troubled by misfortunes, but even in distress remains blessed' (*De Jacob* 1, 28). Or, as Tertullian had said, 'Hunger can have no terror for him who is ready to die with Christ'.

We do, then, perceive a tendency in leading early Christian thinkers firstly, to talk about Christian moral teaching in terms of 'law', secondly, to think of this 'law' as punitive and corrective, and thirdly, to ascribe to the Church the widest powers in discovering and enunciating this 'law'. Given these factors, an increasing specification of Church moral teaching marked by increasing strictness was only to be expected. Such strictness was understandable and a logical consequence of scriptural emphasis on mortification and self-control. But the following observations should be made. They have been stated or implied at various points already in this chapter but since they touch on a basic issue it will be useful to bring them together here. The basic issue is that of the relation of law and morality. In the first place, law and morality are two distinct fields. An important distinction that must be made is that between the 'external' character of law and the 'internal' character of morals. The purpose of law cannot go beyond external conformity. Legal precepts can only be external; they are something different from the inwardness of moral conviction. Moreover, positive law has a coercive character. But coercion destroys the very essence of morality. And if morality involves nothing beyond obeying the law, the Pharisee would be the ideal moral agent. Again, a law can be made as a temporary measure about something that is morally neutral. Yet care must be exercised in framing such laws and seeing that they are not unduly oppressive. For if they are, they will not be observed. And a spirit of disrespect for the laws will grow both from this and from the constant chopping and changing which may be done to remedy the oppressiveness. The same thing will happen in the moral sphere. Finally, but most importantly, the assumption that proclamation of belief in God implies an acquaintance with his mind which can be specified in advance for all particular situations would, if allowed, commit such control to the privileged over the consciences of others who believe in God that it must be submitted to the closest possible examination.

After examination the assumption will of course be rejected. But there is no indication that the assumption was rejected in this form in the centuries that elapsed between Ambrose and Augustine and the rise of canon law. In the first place, they were not centuries rich in thought of any kind. And secondly, the tendency to legalize morals has its attractions: it provides at least certainty. It was natural that men should seek such certainty from the Church. Grace perfects nature, and therefore what is best for human nature will be provided by the Church. The *Decretum Gratiani* (c. 1140), the oldest collection of Church law, is not saying anything new when it maintains: 'Mankind is ruled by two laws: Natural Law and Custom. Natural Law is that which is contained in the Scriptures and the Gospel'. This was simply taking over the teaching attributed to Isidore of Seville (d.636). '*Ius naturale* is that which is contained in the law and the Gospel, by which each is commanded to do to the other what he would have done to himself and is forbidden to do to another what he would not have done to himself.'

The true human teaching was therefore included in the divine teaching. No one was inclined to make a close critical examination of a theory which was so evidently helpful. Nor did it seem necessary to ask whether 'divine' natural law included 'human' natural law in the sense of having added to it as regards content and specific precepts. As God was superior to man, so it was obvious that 'divine' natural law was superior to 'human' natural law. The divine natural law was, also obviously, in the keeping of the Church. Therefore, the more the Church's law was formed, the more also the divine law was formed.

The Church's law was formed increasingly as canon law. The Church's canon law was inspired to a great extent by revived Roman law, and gave full play to its notion of natural law. The *Digest* in Justinian's *Corpus Iuris Civilis* (533 A.D.) begins by quoting the views of the more famous Roman jurists on the nature of law. *Ius civile, gentium* and *naturale* are distinguished. We do not need to concern ourselves with the place and time of origin of this distinction. The point is that for the Middle Ages it was taken as the teaching of the Roman jurists, and they were seen to be teaching that the law of nature (*ius naturale*) corresponds to that which is always good and equitable (*quod semper aequum ac bonum est*). For the Roman jurists *ius naturale* was not, of course, 'a complete system of rules, but a means of interpretation'. But the beginnings of the movement to turn it into a complete set of rules can be seen in the *Decretum Gratiani*. And canon law did in fact become, as Pollock said, the principal vehicle in the Middle Ages of the doctrine of the law of nature. That, however, is another story. How important the story is can only be suggested by recalling that up to the time of Gratian canon law was regarded simply as a part of theology and even when it emerged as a separate discipline it never quite abandoned the notion that it was the word of God. And many canonists would have been happy to see their life's work as an attempt to make God's law (which was also the natural law) of service to man by specifying it, through their interpretation of the wisdom of the Church. Whether this attempt could possibly be a part of God's plan and whether all the results were of service to man, must be left for others to judge.

This chapter has indicated three areas where, as it seems to me, pagan philosophy in an important manner influenced the expression of Christian ethics. These were a Platonic conception of truth, the notion of Christ as the *Logos,* and the natural law tradition. These we have seen to be closely related, with their meeting-place in the notion of Christ as the *Logos.* This is the nodal point because Christianity's chief ethical task must be to present practically and effectively the power of a person, Christ, and its chief problem is deciding how best to do this in words or formulae. For this person was Christianity's real contribution to ethics, and persons are not easily captured in words.

There had been great individuals in the world before Christ and the good man had been offered as the standard of conduct by philosophers before his time. But Christ was something different. His attraction was much more universal than that of anyone who had preceded him. The record of his life made it obvious that he treated all men as equal, saw them as they were as individuals, and was not impressed by superiority of rank, civil or priestly. His message was not one that could be grasped by intellectuals alone, and his importance was not that of a moral philosopher, advancing human understanding by the fineness of his distinctions. His teaching was important because his life was the guarantee of its authenticity. He involved the emotions and it was his personality, rather than subtle expositions of the law, which has held the imagination of all, even non-Christians, ever since.

We react, of course, to the expectations of someone we love even if they are not expressed in words: we think what he would do in such and such a situation, and what he would advise *us* to do in a similar situation. The reaction of someone we love helps us to be more objective on such an occasion, the thought of him inspires us to get beyond our own selfishness, and the memory of him sustains us in carrying out whatever it is we have undertaken. Individual Christians have done great things for humanity, not because they were bound by a law to do them, but because they thought that it was what Christ, whom they loved, would have done if he were in their place.

But it is a human reaction also to want to organize such an

awareness of a person and systematize it. If we think something is good we want to fix it firmly and hold on to it. This is a natural and necessary reaction and it is one of the conditions of intellectual progress: we must think about ethical problems. But the attempt to construct a system brings with it its own danger which intellectuals in particular should be, but often are not, aware of. It is the temptation that Plato succumbed to: he was so impressed by Socrates' moral attitudes that he would have liked to reduce them to propositions that would control the details of all moral behaviour. It would follow from this that the more specific an ethical theory is, the better it is.

This is a dangerous notion. It is also a seductive one, and one that some of the world's greatest thinkers have held. Plato developed his own totalitarian theory from the laudable desire of accounting for and perpetuating the fascination of Socrates' obvious ethical superiority. We might expect the Church to organize and systematize its awareness of Christ because it wants to ensure his continued influence on moral teaching. But in so doing it should never forget the warning of Aristotle, Plato's greatest pupil and severest critic, when he insists that ethics is not an exact science: 'Our discussion will be adequate, if we make it as clear as the subject-matter permits. The same degree of precision should not be demanded in all inquiries . . . We must be content, then, in dealing with this subject, to indicate the truth in broad outline . . . It is the mark of an educated man to seek precision in each kind of inquiry just so far as the nature of the subject permits. It is as inappropriate to demand demonstration in ethics as it is to allow a mathematician to use probable arguments' (*Ethica Nicomachea* 1094b 11 f.).

P. J. McGrath

NATURAL LAW AND MORAL ARGUMENT

There are two ways of looking at an ethical theory. It can be looked at (a) as an account of the central concepts of ethics, that is, as an explanation of what it means to judge an action to be morally good or bad or morally right or wrong; and (b) as providing a pattern for valid argument in ethics. This second aspect will appear more clearly if we point to the parallel between a theory of ethics and a system of logic. The treatment of the syllogism in Aristotelian logic tells us which patterns of syllogistic argument are to be accepted and which to be rejected. Now an ethical theory does the same thing for ethical argument; it tells us which ethical arguments are to be accepted as valid and which to be regarded as invalid. If you accept Utilitarianism in ethics, for example, then you will regard as valid arguments of the form, 'This action or type of action is conducive to the greater happiness of the greater number: therefore it is morally good'; and you will reject as invalid the type of argument which is put forward by, say, natural law moralists or by those who accept hedonism in ethics.

This second way of looking at an ethical theory is one which normally doesn't attract much attention. The reason is that most ethical theories leave little or no room for doubt as to which type of ethical argument they permit and which type they reject. We may not be absolutely clear about the concept of happiness, for example, but at the same time we are sufficiently clear about it to know with certainty that certain types of action are conducive to the general happiness and certain types of action are not. And the same would be true of the concept of pleasure. This brings me to two points which I wish to make about natural law ethics. The first is that the natural law theory is an exception to the general rule we have just been discussing, that is to say, the natural law theory as it has been traditionally understood does not make clear which types of ethical argument the theory commits you to accept or to reject. The second point is that natural law moralists have not been aware of this, or at least have been insufficiently aware of it, with the result that the standard of argumentation within the natural law tradition has been and, I think, is, very unsatisfactory. It will be more convenient if I deal with the second of these points first.

I

If you examine the sort of reasoning employed by moralists in the natural law tradition, one thing that will strike you is the wide variety of argument that natural law moralists are prepared to accept. You might say, of course, that this is one of the virtues of natural law morality, for after all human nature is a complex reality and therefore ethical reasoning must of necessity be complex as well. This sounds reasonable, but there is another side to the coin – the greater the variety of reasoning one is prepared to accept in ethics the greater the necessity for being clear as to the sort of reasoning one is not prepared to accept and the greater the necessity for being clear on the relative merits of different types of ethical argument. Otherwise we will be unable to decide which ethical arguments have genuine force and which have not; and furthermore when the situation arises where you have different arguments pro and contra the same moral principle, there will be no means of deciding the relative merits of these arguments. But there is little evidence that natural law moralists have been clear on these points and a good deal of evidence pointing in the opposite direction.

The first item of evidence is this: There is considerable disagreement amongst natural law moralists as to why certain courses of action are morally wrong. For example, there seem to be at least four different opinions concerning the fundamental reason why lying is immoral. It is claimed to be immoral (a) because it frustrates the function of the faculty of speech which is to communicate truth;[1] (b) because words are naturally signs of thoughts and whoever lies violates the natural bond between a sign and the thing signified;[2] (c) because a lie violates the right of the person spoken to;[3] and (d) because lying frustrates a universal human appetite.[4] You find the same situation with regard to suicide. Some say it is wrong because it violates the rights of the creator;[5] others because it is contrary to the natural human inclination to self-preservation;[6] and finally some say it is wrong because of its bad effects on society.[7]

One could attempt to explain away these discrepancies by saying that these arguments complement rather than exclude each other. But I do not think that this explanation is adequate. For while they do complement each other when considered simply as reasons why lying or suicide is immoral, when considered as basic or fundamental reasons they *are* incompatible. Moreover when you speak of these arguments as complementing each other, you are envisaging a situation where an action is

1. Cf. Noldin-Schmitt, *Summa Theologiae Moralis*, II, 578. The references which I give here and in the following pages are, of course, merely sample ones.

2. Cf. St Thomas, *S. theol.*, IIa IIae, q.110, art.3.

3. H. Grotius, *De Iure Belli et Pacis*, I.iii, c.i., nn.II.

4. Cf. C. Fay, 'Human Evolution: A Challenge to Thomistic Ethics', in *International Philosophical Quarterly* (2) 1960, 66. Natural law moralists usually argue that lying is also wrong because of its evil effects on society, but I have found no one putting this forward as the basic reason for the immorality of lying.

5. Cf. Noldin-Schmitt, *op. cit.*, II, 309.

6. Cf. Joseph Rickaby, *Moral Philosophy*, London 1918, 215-16.

7. Cf. W. Palely, *Ethics*, c.X, n.3, p.178.

wrong for a number of different reasons. But this is possible only of individual actions, whereas what we are concerned with here, since we are dealing with universal moral principles, are types or species of actions. An individual act can be morally wrong for a number of reasons, since it may belong to several moral species at once. The same individual act can involve both a lie and the breaking of a promise, for example. But a morally wrong species as such cannot be morally wrong for a number of reasons for this would mean that it was simultaneously both one species and several species. Of course, there is nothing to prevent you speaking of a class or species of actions which belong simultaneously to two or more moral species. But the point is that if we were considering the morality of such a 'mixed' species, we would first of all have to consider the morality of each 'unmixed' species separately. And here the consideration which I have been arguing for would apply, namely, that each species, if morally wrong, would be morally wrong for one fundamental reason. Or to put this in natural law terms, if a species of actions is contrary to nature, then it is contrary to it in a certain specific way. The fact that there is little agreement within the natural law tradition, therefore, as to why lying or suicide is contrary to nature indicates a basic uncertainty as to how the natural law theory works; or, in other words, as to which ethical arguments are good and which bad.

A second item of evidence is the unsatisfactory character of much of the reasoning found in the natural law tradition. Some moral principles are supported by arguments which are scarcely arguments at all but merely reformulations of the principle. This is particularly true of actions such as incest or sodomy which are universally regarded, by Christians at least, as immoral. These actions are often said to be immoral simply because they are contrary to the order of nature or the rule of right reason; and this is only a concealed way of saying that they are immoral because they are immoral. It may be that the universal agreement concerning these actions means that moralists are rather careless in formulating arguments about them;

at the same time, if it is obvious that these actions are contrary to nature, it ought to be obvious why they are contrary to nature, and this doesn't seem to be the case. Moreover, you occasionally find arguments from reason in the manuals which seem to have no connection with natural law – for example, the argument that lying is immoral on the grounds that it is repugnant to a divine attribute.[8] Apart from the merits of this argument, it is very difficult to see how you could connect it with natural law. Finally, many of the central natural law arguments are open to serious criticism. This is a point I must assume for the moment, since I want to postpone discussion of it until later on. But it all adds up to the suspicion that natural law moralists tend to regard actions as contrary to nature because they already regard them as immoral; and hence that their arguments are really rationalizations rather than genuine arguments.

It would be foolish to think that there is just one single explanation for the unsatisfactory state of the argumentation within the natural law tradition. One factor is that many of these moralists were theologians rather than philosophers and when they had what they believed to be a convincing argument from revelation in favour of a moral principle, they took little care in formulating the argument from reason. A second factor is the uniformity of opinion within the natural law tradition concerning the content of morality. When certain conclusions are universally accepted in a particular field of inquiry, there is little stimulus to examine critically the arguments on which these conclusions are based. It is like the emperor's clothes – if everyone accepts an opinion, nobody bothers to take a critical look at the evidence on which the opinion is based. This factor has obviously influenced the history of the Church's teaching on contraception. So long as the Church's stand was universally accepted by Catholics, there was no pressure on moralists to examine critically the arguments on which that stand was based. It was only after they began to doubt the truth of the Church's teaching that Catholics began to find flaws in the arguments.

8. Cf. Noldin-Schmitt, *op. cit.*, II, 579.

And if we hadn't begun to entertain these doubts, we would probably still be happy with the arguments because we would never have bothered to think seriously about them. Now the greater part of the Church's teaching on morality is still immune from the sort of doubt which has arisen concerning her teaching on contraception. The result is that the Catholic moralist doesn't have to worry unduly about the standards of his argumentation in those areas. Since he knows that his readers won't question the truth of his conclusions, he can safely presume that they won't question the validity of his arguments.

But the principal reason for the unsatisfactory standard of natural law argumentation is, I think, something other than this. It is rather the fact that the natural law theory, unlike other ethical theories, does not make clear which types of ethical argument are valid and which are not. And hence acceptance of the theory does not make clear to moralists which forms of ethical argument they are committed to employ and which to reject. If we look at the natural law theory for a moment we will see why this is so. The natural law, as it has been traditionally understood, is an aspect of the eternal law of God; it is, in other words, that part of God's entire plan for creation which applies to man. The natural law theory, therefore, is based on an analogy between 'law' as it is understood by the physicist or chemist or biologist and 'law' as it is understood by the moralist. The irrational part of creation in obeying the laws of physical nature and man in obeying the laws of his rational nature are both carrying out the divine plan.

Exponents of natural law make it quite clear, of course, that this analogy is only an analogy and not a strict parallel. As St Thomas puts it, rational creatures participate in the eternal law in a manner which is quite different from that of irrational creatures, since they obey it consciously and freely, whereas irrational creatures obey it unconsciously and of necessity. At one crucial point, however, this analogy breaks down completely, that is, when the question arises of our knowledge of the eternal law. We can discover the eternal law for irrational creation by

purely empirical methods. When we know how irrational creatures actually behave, we know how they ought to behave or
how God wants them to behave, since the two things are identical. But how are we to discover how man ought to behave?
Not by seeing how he actually behaves, since unless we already
knew how he ought to behave, we would have no means of
knowing whether his actual behaviour was morally good or bad.
Well, then, how are we to find out how man ought to behave?
Natural law moralists answered this question by saying that we
find out how man ought to behave by seeing how his nature is
constituted. The trouble with this, however, is that there is a
logical gap between the facts about man's nature and the moral
principles which tell us what he ought to do. Natural law moralists found various ways of bridging this gap, but none of these
ways were actually implied by the natural law theory. Consequently one could accept the theory and accept or reject as one
pleased these ways of bridging the gap between human nature
and the moral law, or even produce new ways if one wished.
And this, I believe, is the fundamental reason why there is so
much unsatisfactory reasoning in the natural law tradition and
so many oddly divergent ways of justifying even such an
elementary principle as 'Lying is morally wrong'.

I have said that the analogy between the eternal law as found
in man and as found in irrational creatures breaks down when
we come to explain how we acquire a knowledge of these laws.
But I must qualify this by adding that natural law moralists
would not admit that the analogy breaks down at this point and
St Thomas goes to some pains to show how the analogy can be
understood to continue. For St Thomas every instance of the
eternal law, whether in man or in irrational creation, is an
expression of a natural tendency.[9] If water invariably boils at
100° centigrade or material bodies are attracted towards each
other by the force which we call gravity, this is because they
have a natural tendency to behave in this way. Similarly, if
man ought to speak the truth or ought not commit suicide, this

9. Cf. *S. theol.*, Ia IIae, q.1, art.6.

is because he has a natural tendency towards truth or towards the preservation of his life. For St Thomas man has three basic natural tendencies.[10] As a substance he has a natural tendency towards self-preservation and it is from this that the moral principles concerning the preservation of life are derived. As animal he has a natural tendency towards reproduction and this provides the basis for moral principles concerning sex and family life. Finally, as a rational being he has a natural tendency towards truth and towards life in society and from this derive the moral principles which govern his social life.

The question which we must raise at this point is: Does this concept of 'natural tendency' enable St Thomas to successfully bridge the gap between human nature as it is and human behaviour as it ought to be; in other words, does the natural law theory as understood in the light of this concept of 'natural tendency' commit you to accepting certain forms of ethical argument as valid and rejecting others as invalid? The answer to this question must, I think, be 'No'. For how are we to know what are man's natural tendencies? The only possible answer is that we discover what they are by looking at man's behaviour, just as we learn the natural tendencies of irrational creatures by looking at the manner in which they behave. But observation of human behaviour might lead us to conclude that man has a natural tendency to lie, or to drink, too much, or to oppress his fellow man. We are faced then with the old difficulty that before reaching conclusions about the content of natural law, we will be unable to distinguish in human behaviour between what is moral and what is immoral and therefore unable to base a morality on the tendencies which we find there.

St Thomas's classification of human natural tendencies seems to owe as much to the tree of Porphyry as to empirical investigation. But no one these days expects nature to subscribe to the canons of definition *per genus et differentiam*. Modern psychologists provide rather different classifications of the basic human drives or tendencies. According to Freud in his later period, for

10. Cf. *S. theol.*, Ia IIae, q.94, art.2.

example, the two fundamental human tendencies are the life instinct and the death instinct, eros and thanatos. According to Adler, the basic human tendency is the will to power or to self-assertion. If you accepted one of these theories and also accepted St Thomas's conception of the ethical significance of the basic human tendencies, then you would arrive, I feel, at some very odd ethical conclusions.

St Thomas himself does not seem to have taken this part of ethical theory very seriously, since if he had, he should have appealed to it in all his ethical arguments; an action for him should be morally good only if it accords with a natural tendency and morally bad only if it frustrates a natural tendency. But in fact he uses several other forms of ethical argument in his writings and I have been able to find only three instances where he uses this type of ethical argument explicitly – to show that love of one's neighbour is morally good, to show that sexual intercourse is morally good and to show that suicide is morally wrong. So I think we can conclude that St Thomas was aware of the difficulties in his own position.

II

I now wish to examine the various ways in which natural law moralists tried to span the gap between human nature as it is actually constituted and human behaviour as it ought to be, or, what amounts to the same thing, the principal forms of ethical argument found in the natural law tradition. There seem to be four main types at least – (1) the argument based on natural tendencies; (2) the argument from consequences; (3) the argument based on the natural function or purpose of a faculty; and (4) the argument from rights. This classification is not, of course, exhaustive; there are other forms of argument used, but these are either eccentric or exceptional and need not, therefore, be considered here. It is worth mentioning here that the second and third of these forms of argument were employed in the encyclical *Humanae Vitae*. I will now examine each of these four main types of argument in turn.

(1) The first type is the argument from natural tendencies. We have already pointed out the difficulty of deciding which are man's natural tendencies. But even if we overlook this point and presume that we have an accurate list of man's natural tendencies, further difficulties arise. If something is good or bad because it is in accordance with or contrary to a natural tendency, and if the natural tendency is in human nature because God has implanted it there, does it not follow that the action is good or bad because God has willed or forbidden it? For example if, as St Thomas argues,[11] love of neighbour is good because men have a natural tendency to love one another, wouldn't it follow that love of neighbour would be morally indifferent or even morally bad if God had implanted a different or contrary instinct in human nature? And this conclusion is obviously unacceptable. One could perhaps argue that the basic human tendencies follow of necessity from human nature and that therefore God had no choice in creating man but to implant these tendencies in him. But this would mean that the objects of these tendencies are not necessarily morally good. Every finite being endowed with free will might have, of necessity, a natural tendency to do wrong – if one were inclined to argue in this way, there would be no lack of empirical evidence to support one's position. So it seems that the natural tendency argument avoids ethical voluntarism only at the expense of depriving natural tendencies of their ethical significance.

In any event, natural tendencies seem incapable of bearing all the weight which moralists place upon them. For example, it seems impossible to understand how the natural tendency to reproduction could provide an adequate basis for a coherent sexual morality; if our sexual morality was really based on that tendency, wouldn't fornication be far more moral than celibacy?

---

11. See *Summa Contra Gentes*, Book III, ch. CXVII.

Or take the argument that lying is immoral because it frustrates
the natural appetite for truth. But if I lie, I don't frustrate *my*
appetite for truth, but somebody else's. So to complete the
argument, one must introduce into human nature a natural
tendency not to frustrate the natural tendencies of others. And
at this stage the argument is in danger of becoming ridiculous;
one could legitimately appeal to a variant of Ockham's razor –
natural tendencies are not to be multiplied beyond necessity.

(2) The second type of argument is the argument from consequences. This is used in all sorts of different contexts by natural
law moralists and it is also employed by the encyclical *Humanae
Vitae* (see paragraph 17), though it is not easy to judge
how much weight the Pope attaches to it. The form of the
argument is as follows: Lying or suicide or contraception is
immoral because if they are not and people are free to indulge
in these practices as they please, the effect on society will be
disastrous. One thing that should make us suspicious about this
type of argument is that if it is valid, then many practices which
are normally regarded as innocent should in fact be regarded as
immoral – smoking, for instance, or driving a car or taking a
drink. When one remembers that approximately sixty thousand
people are killed each year in road accidents in Western Europe
and that most of these deaths would be avoided if cars were
kept off the roads, then it is easy to see that there is a consequences argument against driving which is at least as strong as
the parallel argument against suicide or contraception. But this
example also shows the weakness of this type of argumentation.
For even though car driving has such horrifying consequences
for humanity, this does not mean that every time one drives,
one is behaving immorally. The fact that a certain type of
action will sometimes be performed irresponsibly does not
mean that every action of that type is morally wrong. The
medievals summed this up in a neat phrase: *Abusus non tollit
usum*. Even though a thing be abused by some, this does not
prevent it from being properly used by others.

Has this type of argument then any part to play in ethics?

The answer, I think, must be 'No', though it would be difficult to provide a complete justification for this view without drawing distinctions between different types of actions and different types of moral situations. Without going into this detail, however, one can, I think, say this: if the consequences argument is ever valid, it is because the doing of an action will induce others to do the same and the effect of this on society as a whole will be bad. But I do not think that this sort of argument could ever be validly used in ethics. For the effect on society will be bad only if some of these actions have bad consequences in themselves and therefore are immoral in themselves independently of whether they induce others to perform the same sort of action or not. But if the original action was of this type, then the consequences argument does not apply, since the original action is already immoral even if it does not induce others to do the same. But if it is not of this type, then we have no reason for thinking that it will induce others to perform the same action in such a way as to produce bad consequences. For how could the responsible performance of an action induce others to perform the same action irresponsibly? How could driving a car carefully, for instance, induce others to drive dangerously? One can, I suppose, conceive of this sort of thing happening, but it would certainly be an extraordinary occurrence and one which could not be used as the basis for a conclusion about the effects of driving in general.

The proponents of the consequences argument were obviously thinking, though not perhaps explicitly, along these lines: If I drive, I induce others to drive and since some of these are bound to drive dangerously, it follows that I cannot drive at all without inducing others to drive dangerously. But this argument is quite clearly invalid. One might as well argue that if I speak the truth, I induce others to tell lies, since if I speak at all, I thereby induce others to speak also and some of them are bound to speak falsely. It is clear, therefore, that if an action is performed responsibly, the consequences argument cannot be used against it to show that it is immoral, whereas if it is not performed responsibly, it is immoral in any case and appeal to the consequences argument is superfluous.

The use of this type of argument in the encyclical *Humanae Vitae* exposes its weaknesses. For if, as the encyclical claims, artificial contraception is wrong in itself, that is, independently of its consequences for society, the consequences argument is irrelevant, since *ex hypothesi* it is not its consequences which make contraception morally wrong. If on the other hand contraception is not wrong in itself, then we have no reason for assuming that the responsible use of contraceptive methods will lead others to use them irresponsibly, and therefore no reason for thinking that contraception is immoral because of its consequences for society. So the consequences argument is either irrelevant or invalid. The encyclical's position on consequences is particularly weak since it is based on the unspoken assumption that those who would disobey the Pope were he to allow the use of the pill in certain well-defined circumstances within marriage, will obey him now that he has outlawed it completely; one has only to state this assumption to see how improbable it is. One might claim, of course, that the Pope is not really using the consequences argument, but merely asking his readers to contemplate the consequences of contraception for society so that they may be more easily convinced of its immorality. But even this presupposes the validity of the consequences argument, for otherwise how could contemplation of the consequences lead one to think that contraception is morally wrong?

The consequences argument could be validly used in a non-ethical context when it is a question of someone imposing a rule or a positive law. And its use in ethics is, I think, due to a confusion between the role of the legislator and the role of the moralist. A legislator could legitimately argue that a whole class of actions should be outlawed, not because each individual instance is harmful, but because this is the only way of preventing harmful actions of this type from being performed; this is what happens when a speed-limit is imposed, for example. But the moralist cannot argue that he should declare a certain type of action to be immoral, for otherwise great harm will ensue. As a moralist he is not entitled to forbid or sanction anything, as is the legislator. His job is to make a judgement, not a decision; and the effects of his judgement are no more relevant to its truth than the effects of a declaration in favour of the Copernican theory would be to the truth of the proposition that the earth goes around the sun.

(3) The third type of argument is based on the purpose or function of human faculties. This type of argument is normally used by natural law moralists in dealing with sexual morality and the morality of lying. It is also the main argument appealed to by the encyclical *Humanae Vitae*, though it is formulated there in an unusual way (par. 12).[12] The word 'meaning' (*significatio*) is used instead of 'function' or 'purpose', but this, I think, is an effort to forestall criticism that it is viewing sex in a purely biological manner. This type of argument faces some of the difficulties of the argument from natural tendencies. For how do we know what is the natural function of a faculty? The argument on lying claims that the function of the faculty of speech is to communicate truth. This seems to be based on the assumption that when we speak, we invariably utter propositions – expressions which are either true or false. But many, perhaps most, of the things we say are not intended to be propositions; they are requests, questions, wishes, jokes, prayers, exhortations, commands, exclamations, insults and so on. None of these set out to be either true or false, so it is difficult to see how one could seriously defend the view that *the* function of the faculty is to communicate truth. Couldn't one make a more plausible

12. In an article entitled 'The Arguments of *Humanae Vitae*' (*The Month*, March 1969, p. 151) Timothy Potts says that the central argument of the encyclical is 'completely new and has not appeared in the literature before'. But this sounds most implausible. One can hardly accept that in paragraph 12 Pope Paul is claiming that the traditional teaching of the Church on contraception is based on an argument which has never previously been put forward. Moreover, in paragraph 13 the encyclical speaks of the meaning and purpose (*significatio et finis*) of sexual intercourse as if the terms were synonymous.

case for saying that the function of speech was originally to enable man to survive? If you accept this, the argument against lying collapses. Or take the sex-faculty. Couldn't one make a plausible case for the view that one of its functions is to give pleasure? And if so, couldn't one develop a natural law argument in favour of various types of behaviour which Christians invariably regard as morally wrong.

In his *Philosophical Investigations* Wittgenstein explained why philosophers so readily accepted a certain error in philosophy by saying, 'A picture held us captive' (par. 115). Natural law moralists in putting forward arguments of this form were, I think, held captive by a picture, a picture of man's faculties as delicate instruments fashioned for a particular purpose by the creator. This led them to think of lying or the misuse of the sex-faculty as equivalent to using, say, a surgical instrument to pare a pencil. Now this picture of man's faculties is, I believe, inadequate for two reasons. In the first place it is inadequate for the purpose for which natural law moralists employ it. Using a surgical instrument to pare a pencil makes it unfit for use as a surgical instrument, but using the faculty of speech to tell a lie won't prevent you from telling the truth in future. In other words, the picture demands that misuse of the faculty renders it either defective or useless as far as its proper use is concerned, whereas the misuse moralists are thinking of is merely the using it for a purpose other than that for which it is intended. And so even granted the picture, their arguments are defective. Secondly, the picture is, in any event, the wrong picture. Human nature and the human faculties were not directly created by God as the medievals believed; they have evolved. The human species has, in a certain sense, grown from very lowly origins. Hence if you want to compare man and his faculties with human artefacts, you must compare them, not with things such as watches or pens or surgical instruments, but rather with a city or an institution which has grown to be what it is through a lengthy process of change and adaptation and development. And once you change the picture, the faculty argument disintegrates. For if you depart from the original plan of a city or institution, you are not necessarily going against the will of the founding fathers; what you are doing now may be precisely what they themselves would have done in similar circumstances. In the same way, if man alters the functioning of his faculties, he is not necessarily going against the will of his creator, since alteration and adaptation have been going on in nature from the very beginning.

(4) The fourth argument is the argument from rights. Again this is used in a variety of contexts by natural law moralists – in connection with property, with suicide, with the worship due to God and so on. The form of the argument is that an action is wrong because it violates the rights of another, whether the other is God, another person or society in general. There is another sort of argument, connected with this, which you occasionally find in the natural law manuals. This is that an action is wrong because it involves treating a person, not as a person, but as a thing. Fundamentally, I think, the two arguments are the same, since when you respect a person's rights, you treat him as a person, and when you ignore his rights, you reduce him to the level of a thing. Rights are an expression of personality from the moral point of view. But what is so remarkable about this argument is that it is so very different from the others which we have been considering. For in the other arguments you were arguing from an 'is' to an 'ought', from the purpose of a faculty or the existence of a natural tendency or the effects on society of some course of action to the judgement that something ought or ought not to be done. The premises of these arguments were certain facts which were in themselves ethically neutral; the difficulty was to give these facts an ethical significance and it was on this difficulty that these arguments foundered. But this problem does not arise in connection with this fourth argument. For the facts on which this argument is based are of themselves ethically significant; they have an 'ought' built into them so that there is no logical gap to be bridged in drawing an ethical conclusion from them. To say that someone

has a right is *eo ipso* to say that others ought to respect that right; if it does not say that, then to say that someone has a right is to say nothing at all.

There is a second way in which this fourth argument differs from the other three. The others place man on the same level as the rest of creation. They see man as a being with natural tendencies, with certain faculties each of which has a particular purpose and whose actions may have an effect on the entire group. Now there is nothing specifically human about all this; these features are also found in irrational creation. And, of course, this is part of the natural law way of looking at man; it sees him as governed by a code of laws which applies to creation as a whole. But when you begin to argue from rights and from personality, you are immediately on a different level. For rights and personality are what mark man off from the rest of creation; he is the only being in creation who is a person, who possesses rights. And once you realize this, you have to ask yourself whether this argument is really compatible with the natural law theory as it has been traditionally understood. And I think you would have to say, 'No, it isn't'. If you accept this type of argument, then to be consistent you must reconstruct the natural law theory and place at its centre not the concept of nature, but the concept of person.

III

What form then should ethical arguments take? To answer this question satisfactorily one would need to write a full-scale treatise on ethics. But without going this far one can, I believe, lay down certain rules to which ethical argumentation must conform if it is to have any claim to be valid. The first is that moral judgements, whether they are general or particular, always need supporting arguments or reasons. Moral judgements are not like judgements of sense perception. We cannot perceive moral attributes like rightness or wrongness as we perceive qualities such as redness or whiteness and it cannot happen therefore that one could know that something was right or wrong without having any reason for one's view. (This is not to be confused with having a reason without being able to articulate it, or with the situation where there are reasons for and against the rightness of an action and one knows intuitively that one reason outweighs the other.) To know that something is right or wrong one needs criteria for the application of these terms and these criteria constitute the supporting reasons for the moral judgement. If, for example, you say that an action is wrong because it involves stealing, you are using as a criterion for the application of the term 'wrong' the fact that the action involved the taking of property against its owner's wishes. And you are arguing implicitly in this way: Whatever involves stealing is wrong (other things being equal). This involves stealing; therefore this is wrong.

There is one important corollary from this: appeal to authority is never sufficient justification for a moral judgement. This does not mean that someone might not be justified in acting on a moral principle which he accepts from authority rather than sees the truth of himself. What it does mean is that the authority must itself have a reason for its moral judgement and its opinions on moral matters are no better than the reasons which underlie them. This seems to undermine one line of approach to the teaching on contraception in *Humanae Vitae*, that of those who say that while they cannot accept the Pope's reasons, they accept his teaching, since it was delivered under divine guidance. But since grace works through nature, would not divine guidance on moral matters necessarily take the form of enabling one to perceive the reasons why some course of action is right or wrong? It does not make sense to say that the divine guidance extended only as far as the judgement and left untouched the reasons on which the judgement was based, since the making of the judgement and the reasoning which underlies it are all part of the same process. Since one cannot accept, therefore, that the holy Spirit aided the Pope to make the right judgement for the wrong reasons, if one accepts his judgement, one must also accept his reasons or provide better reasons in their place.

The second rule to which moral reasoning must conform is that the reasoning which underlies a moral judgement must be deductive in character. This follows from what we have said about criteria, since to apply a moral predicate in accordance with a criterion is implicitly to appeal to a more general moral principle; to say that something is wrong because it is x is to make implicit appeal to the principle, 'Everything which is x is wrong'. Nevertheless the deductive character of moral reasoning is something which has come to be questioned by Catholic moralists, but this is partly due, I think, to the undue stress on deductive reasoning in traditional Catholic moral theology, where it was sometimes assumed that the conclusions of the moralist were as clear-cut as those of the geometrician. There can be no doubt that deduction by itself is not sufficient for arriving at ethical conclusions, since particular moral problems often involve a conflict of principles and can be resolved, not by deduction, but by what Aristotle called 'perception', something akin to good taste in artistic matters. But deduction is, I believe, the only possible way in which we could arrive at general moral principles, though the deduction here will not possess the lucidity of deductive reasoning in logic or in mathematics. If you do not accept this view, then the only alternative is to hold that moral principles are arrived at by induction, a view which has recently been put forward by John Coventry.[13] This would mean adopting an intuitionist theory of moral judgement, since if we do not use criteria for the application of terms such as 'right' or 'wrong', then the only way for us to recognize rightness or wrongness is through some form of intuition; if our recognition of moral attributes is not indirect, it must be either direct or non-existent. The weakness of intuitionist ethics has, however, been very fully exposed in recent English moral philosophy and anyone adopting an intuitionist theory of moral

13. See John Coventry 'Christian Conscience', *The Heythrop Journal* (VII) 1966, 145-60.

judgement has a great many objections to answer before his position can be taken seriously, a task which has so far not been taken on by any supporter of ethical inductivism.

Besides even if we overlook the weakness of intuitionism, it does not seem possible to form moral principles by means of induction. Any action may be described in various ways, and if it is immoral it won't necessarily be immoral under every description. Oswald's action in killing Kennedy, for example, was wrong not because he pressed the trigger, or released the spring, or fired the gun, though these are all accurate descriptions of what he did from different points of view, but because he deliberately killed a man. If you condemn an action morally and are unable to state under which description it is morally blameworthy, you will be unable to use that judgement as the basis for a general principle; it is no use saying 'All actions belonging to the same class as this action are morally wrong' if you do not know to which class this action belongs. But if you say that this action is wrong because it comes under this description, this is equivalent to saying that it is wrong because it is x. And this is the same thing as saying that you have arrived at this particular judgement because you accept the general principle that all actions which are x are wrong. So it appears there is no room for induction in moral reasoning.

The third rule to which moral reasoning must conform is that it must be concerned in some way with human welfare. An action cannot be morally wrong unless it is humanly bad, that is detrimental to human welfare, and it cannot be morally right unless it is humanly good. There is a passage in the *Summa Contra Gentes* which bears on this point. St Thomas is considering the objection that if two people commit fornication in such circumstances that they do no harm thereby either to themselves or to society, then they cannot be said to have done anything morally wrong. The objection goes on to say: 'Nor does it seem a sufficient answer to say that they wrong God, for God is not offended by us except by what we do against our own good; but it does not appear that this conduct is against man's good; hence no wrong seems to be done to God thereby'.[14] The significant thing is that St Thomas answers this objection on its own terms; he tries to show, in other words, that certain types of sexual behaviour are wrong because they are contrary to man's own good and not for any other reason. But this type of objection has not been taken sufficiently seriously by Catholic moralists since then. They have been shielded from it by the assumption that if an action is contrary to the order of nature, then it is morally wrong whether the order of nature has anything to do with human good or not. This too is the most serious defect in the reasoning which underlies the encyclical's condemnation of contraception. Even when it is discussing the consequences of contraception, it mentions only its bad consequences as if its good consequences were of no account. But this type of objection is one which Catholic morality will have to take more seriously in future.

14. *Summa Contra Gentes*, Book III, ch. CXXII.

CIARAN RYAN

SCIENCE AND MORAL LAW

A significant feature of the encyclical *Humanae Vitae*, and one which has been somewhat overlooked, is the fact that the encyclical is addressed not only to the bishops, priests and faithful of the Roman Catholic Church but also to all men of good will. This, of course, does not represent a new departure but rather carries on a practice initiated by Pope John XXIII. The fact does, however, have important consequences for the discussion of the present encyclical. Basically what it implies is that the teaching of the encyclical is intended to be intelligible to both non-Catholics and Catholics alike. No specifically Catholic considerations are being appealed to and although the teaching may be, in the words of the encyclical, 'founded on the natural law illuminated and enriched by divine revelation' (par. 12), it should in the end be a teaching open to the understanding of all. In view of this it is legitimate to ask how well the encyclical succeeds in its avowed purpose of speaking to all men, or in other words to enquire how in fact its arguments fare when judged by current non-theological thinking. In particular in this article we shall be concerned with the matter of the encyclical viewed in the light of scientific thought and attitudes.

It is scarcely necessary to remark that science occupies a position of very great importance in the world in which we live.

This is true not only because a great part of that world is itself a direct result of science but also because scientific thinking exercises a profound influence on what might be called the general philosophical climate. Scientific thinking in many ways serves as a model of thought and in all spheres one hears of the need to adopt a scientific approach. The enormous prestige enjoyed by science derives ultimately from its success, from its ability to tackle and solve problems in a systematic way. In a world increasingly aware of its own evolutionary character the great attraction of science is not difficult to understand. The question to be answered here is how does *Humanae Vitae* appear to this science-conscious, science-oriented world.

What we are concerned with basically is a question of outlook – an outlook or mentality common to a great number (one might suspect a majority) of people today – according to which science and scientific modes of thought are held in very high regard. Whatever one thinks of it, one cannot deny that this mentality exists. It is emphasized that this mentality does not wish to dictate what shall be said on any particular subject (such as the present one of marital morality); but it is there and has its own validity. Our purpose is to examine how the encyclical will appear in a world where this mentality is so much an accepted part.

We begin with two preliminary observations. The first has to do with the question of authority. It is accepted by all that authority has a rightful place in human affairs and especially would it be conceded that authority legitimately operates in the area of traditional religious faith. But it must also be recognized that people today are simply not prepared to give blanket approval to authoritative statements. For this reason any unsupported appeal to authority on the part of the encyclical would of its nature tend to alienate. The reason here is that in human affairs generally and in the scientific sphere in particular the argument from authority is the weakest of all. It is not the case, as is sometimes stated, that authority has no place in science – it certainly has, as anyone connected with science will testify. However the authority in question is an authority of competence – certain people are regarded as authorities in their particular fields and it would be a foolhardy person indeed who would neglect to consult their work. Yet this kind of authority never guarantees the correctness of the work done; it is rather in the nature of a presumption in favour of the person that his work is in fact correct. Judging by past performance we expect the work of this person on this subject to be correct and valuable; but the correctness and value of the work itself rests ultimately on its own intrinsic merits. It is true of course that of the nature of the case the role and operation of authority will differ considerably in the Church and in science. Nevertheless it is with the scientific model of authority that the modern mind is impressed, with its emphasis on competence. Viewed in this light paragraph 4 of the encyclical, which asserts the right of the teaching authority of the Church to make pronouncements on marital morality, is seen not as a decisive factor in the discussion but rather as the presentation of credentials by an important and highly competent interested party.

A second preliminary observation is that any attempt to prejudge the issue by appeal to existing or past positions would run very contrary to the methods of investigation employed in science. A hallmark of the scientific method has been the spirit of free enquiry and any compromise in this matter would give rise to very serious misgivings. In this connection, even allowing for the greater importance of tradition in the religious field as contrasted with science, it is particularly unfortunate that the reason given in the encyclical for rejecting the recommendations of the Papal Commission for the Study of Problems of Population, Family and Birth is that 'certain criteria of solutions had emerged which departed from the moral teaching on marriage proposed with constant firmness by the teaching authority of the Church' (par. 6). To any scientist this sounds suspiciously like the statement that no new approaches or solutions are acceptable and it is scarcely necessary to say what his opinion of this kind of thinking would be. Clearly such an attitude in science would mean its death. New ideas and new approaches are the life blood of science. This is not to say that there is nothing unchanging in science – in fact there is a broad general framework within which innovations occur. Indeed the history of science is not a history of revolution but of evolution; scientific ideas which have proved valid are not overthrown but rather refined and a crucial test of any new scientific theory is whether it contains within it the valid ingredients of the old. Thus in science the new and the old have each a part to play, the tension between them providing the essential dynamic of the subject. Any attempt to exclude new ideas simply because they are new would be regarded most unfavourably by anyone acquainted with the scientific method.

Turning now to the more central issues it seems that the area where the man of science would find the greatest difficulty with the encyclical would be in its understanding of the nature of physical law and of nature itself. In this connection there are several relevant statements in the encyclical. In paragraph 10 we read: 1. 'In relation to biological processes responsible parenthood means the knowledge and respect for their functions; human intellect discovers in the power of giving life biological laws which are part of the human person.' (Given the rudimentary state of biological knowledge in his day it comes as a surprise to find a reference at this point to St Thomas, *Summa Theologica*, I-II, q.94, art. 2.) In paragraph 11 it is stated that: 2. 'God has wisely disposed natural laws and rhythms of fecundity which, of themselves, cause a separation of births.' Paragraph 12 which asserts the inseparable connection between the unitive and procreative aspects of the conjugal act contains the statement: 3. 'Indeed, by its intimate structure the conjugal act while most closely uniting husband and wife, capacitates them for the generation of new lives according to laws inscribed in the very being of man and woman.' As a final instance we cite paragraph 13 which speaks of the necessity of 'respecting the laws of the generative process'.

Before proceeding further we would like to remark with

regard to quotation 2 above that the only known law which causes a separation in the succession of births is the law of pregnancy according to which successive births are spaced by nine months. Other factors may extend this period but in fact none of them is infallible. There are cases on record of women giving birth ten times in ten years. On this point it is worth quoting from a report of the Bargy Castle meeting on *Humanae Vitae* the following passage:

> The members of the medical profession present stated that the biological premise upon which the encyclical's recommendations of the rhythm method is based is scientifically untenable. The reference to natural laws and rhythms of fecundity which 'iam per se ipsa generationes subsequentes interrallent' was incorrect, and consequently these natural laws and rhythms could not provide the basis for a sufficiently effective method of regulating births.[1]

Reverting now to the passages quoted above and others similar to them, we remark that the encyclical seems at first sight to be resting a great part of its case on biological laws operating in the generative process. (We shall see later that this is only partly true.) Now to a scientist a law of nature is simply a statement about how the world works. Water boils at 100°C. The path of the earth is an ellipse with the sun at one focus. The statement in question may be more or less profound, more or less general but basically it is a statement about the behaviour of the physical world. In particular a law of nature has of itself no moral implications or innuendos. We cannot say, for example, that water must boil at 100°C and that for water to boil at any other temperature is immoral (water can in fact be made to boil at temperatures different from 100°C by altering the pressure upon it). Thus in order to erect a moral precept on

1. *The Furrow*, **November 1968, 657.**

a physical or biological law it is simply not enough to state what the law is.

The second thing about a law of nature is that it is invariably provisional. This is so for two reasons. On the one hand there is always the awareness that you never know the whole story of the workings of the physical world and so the laws you state at any given time are necessarily approximate and subject to revision. There may well be laws inscribed on the face of nature but our understanding of them always remains incomplete and as far as concerns us it is this latter which counts. A law of nature is also provisional in the sense that it holds provided that certain conditions are fulfilled. Water boils at 100°C provided it is at normal atmospheric pressure. The earth describes an ellipse with the sun at one focus provided that forces on it other than that from the sun are negligible. In other words laws of nature are not absolute as regards their operation; their operation can be modified by circumstances or by the presence of other competing laws. In consequence of this it would seem that moral teaching based on such laws should be equally provisional and flexible in its approach.

What has been said so far clearly indicates that laws of nature in so far as we can formulate them are highly idealized statements. In an actual experiment one never finds the law realized exactly either because of the uncertainties involved in the process of measurement or because of the operation of other laws besides that being tested. There is always some degree of discrepancy between the actual workings of the physical world as we observe them and our conceptualization of these workings which we call laws of nature.

In the case of the laws of human reproduction this discrepancy can be very great. It is true that in the process of human reproduction a fairly well-defined pattern or law can be discerned but it is also true that deviations from this pattern in individual cases are both many and substantial. Thus the female cycle lasts on an average twenty-eight days with ovulation occurring on the average on the fourteenth day, yet a well-known textbook on obstetrics can state: 'No woman menstruates quite regularly. In the most regular cases menstruation varies by three or four days, a usual cyclical variation being twenty-five to twenty-eight days ... Greater variations in time and rhythm frequently occur and may occur in one individual with increasing age, change of climate or environment, emotion or between pregnancies.'[2] Regarding the time of ovulation the same text states: 'The most recent work on this subject indicates that the time of ovulation varies within greater limits than was previously thought ... ovulation may occur on any day from day 6 to day 20 with high frequencies from day 12 to day 15'. Thus the laws holding in this area are seen to be of an extremely approximate character. In fact they are laws only in the statistical sense, that is, they describe a uniform behaviour which occurs only on an average with wide fluctuations possible not only from individual to individual but also in one individual herself.

The example just considered clearly illustrates one point, namely that all laws of nature are not of equal standing. Depending on the degree of our understanding, the laws we are able to state in different areas vary considerably in exactness. Usually laws concerning macroscopic behaviour can be stated with a great deal more preciseness and generality than those concerning microscopic behaviour; the law of gravitation is of a much more satisfactory character than the laws of elementary particle interactions.

The relevance of this observation to the present discussion is hinted at in this last remark. The point is that the real value of knowing a law of nature is that it enables one to make predictions. Clearly the kind of predictions which can be made depends on how well the law is known. The law of gravitation is satisfactory because we know it so well that from it we can make predictions of any required accuracy; in the case of elementary particle processes the situation is far from being so. Since the

2. J. F. Cunningham, *Text book of Obstetrics*, 4th ed., London 1964, 14.

laws of human reproduction are at present of such an approximate character their predictive power is correspondingly limited. For this reason the solution to the problem of birth regulation proposed by the encyclical, namely 'the use of marriage in infecund periods only' (par. 16) appears quite unsatisfactory from a scientific standpoint. With the present state of knowledge this solution is simply not adequate.

An important clue as to the thinking which dominates the encyclical can be got from its repeated insistence that a law of nature is something to be respected and followed. Thus responsible parenthood is said to require respect for the functions of biological processes (par. 12) and in using the gift of conjugal love man must respect 'the laws of the generative process' (par. 13). The reason man must respect these laws is that they represent 'the design established by the creator' (par. 13). Now this is an important consideration and must be carefully examined. Taken literally it would reduce man to the position of a mere slave with respect to physical laws. This cannot have been intended since man, while in general going along with these laws, feels free to oppose those which are injurious to him. Examples of this kind of action are the use of lightning conductors to ward off lightning or of vaccines to guard against disease. Thus simply because a law of nature is involved it does not automatically follow that man is forbidden from taking preventative action and consequently an appeal for obedience to laws of nature does not constitute a conclusive argument. What is required is to show that in the laws of the generative process are enshrined moral prescriptions.

This apparently is what the encyclical seeks to do in paragraphs 11 and 12. Here it is stated that the fundamental principle on which the teaching of the Church is based is 'that each and every marriage act must remain open to the transmission of life. That teaching often set forth by the magisterium is founded on the inseparable connection willed by God and unable to be broken by man on his own initiative between the two meanings of the conjugal act: the unitive meaning and the procreative meaning.' This passage has been extensively analysed ever since the encyclical first appeared and it is unnecessary to rehearse the arguments here.[3] Looked at from the scientific viewpoint it is difficult to understand what is meant. As is well known, the great majority of marriage acts are not in fact open to the trans-mission of life due to circumstances such as pregnancy, the onset of menopause, hysterectomy or simply the occurrence of the infertile period. Likewise in these same marriage acts the procreative meaning of the act is quite absent except perhaps in some symbolic sense. Is it that in these sterile unions there can be present a desire to procreate new life even though conditions are not right for that? But is it not also possible to have this same desire present in cases where artificial contraception is employed?

Ultimately, however, it seems that the teaching of the ency-clical hinges on a distinction it draws between what is natural and what artificial in the context of contraception. The lawful-ness of contraception itself, that is of engaging in intercourse while positively excluding conception, has been accepted ever since the pronouncement of Pope Pius XII on the use of the safe period method. However, the teaching has been that only the safe period method is lawful because it alone uses a natural means; all other means are artificial and are therefore rejected. The encyclical says in reference to these two types of means, 'In reality there are essential differences between the two cases: in the former, the married couple make legitimate use of a natural disposition, in the latter they impede the development of a natural process' (par. 16). This of course is true but is it rele-vant? There are numerous cases where development of a natural process is impeded without moral sanction. In fact one might say that everyday life is littered with such cases. On the more trivial side there are things like cutting one's hair or fingernails. More substantial would be something like cosmetic surgery.

---

3. See for example, the article by Lionel Keane in *On Human Life,* Burns Oates, London 1968.

From the very area we are concerned with here we have the extremely relevant example of the use of fertility pills. (Since the action of these pills is just the opposite of that of the most common contraceptive pill – that is to say they stimulate ovulation while the contraceptive pill inhibits it – there is no question but that the amount of intervention involved in the two cases is the same.) We may ask then why is intervention allowed in these cases but not in the case of birth control? This is the crucial question and not whether or not artificial means are used.

The answer of the encyclical on this point is that both in the use of the safe period method and in the use of artificial means 'the married couple are concordant in the positive will of avoiding children for plausible reasons, seeking the certainty that offspring will not arrive; but it is also true that only in the former case are they able to renounce the use of marriage in fecund periods when for just motives procreation is not desirable, while making use of it during infecund periods to manifest their affection and to safeguard their mutual fidelity' (par. 16).

If this passage is not to be taken as a straightforward begging of the question (i.e. as saying that the safe period method is lawful because it is the safe period method) then it involves an appeal to an ascetic ideal according to which it is better to renounce the use of marriage in certain circumstances. Now while it is possible to consider the existence of some such ideal as a general guiding principle in this whole area, the difficulty is that the encyclical imposes this ideal as a norm and it does so without any explanation as to how either ideal or norm was arrived at; the position is justified simply by the statement that those who observe this norm give proof of a truly and integrally honest love. This may be true but the question still remains, 'Is it impossible for those who do not observe this norm to have a truly and integrally honest love?' This question is not answered.

In the end one is left with the conclusion that the central problem has not been solved. (Actually the encyclical gives the impression that it is aware of this itself by the way it keeps changing the ground of its argument from authority to natural law to the natural-unnatural distinction to ascetic considerations.)

Also quite inadequately dealt with is the so-called problem of the population explosion. This problem is stated in paragraph 2 as follows: 'Fear is shown by many that the world population is growing more rapidly than available resources ...' to which might be added the serious implications for the human race of recent findings of behavioural scientists concerning the disruptive effects of overcrowding in animal populations. The answer to this problem offered by the encyclical is for public authorities to have 'a provident policy for the family' and to 'provide a wise education of peoples in respect of the moral law and the liberty of citizens'. Now while there is a considerable difference of opinion regarding the solution of the population problem it is difficult to see how these remarks confront the central issue at all. This issue is the well-known exponential growth law of populations and anyone remotely familiar with it will know how serious the matter is. According to this mathematical law, given the present growth rate the population of the world will double in the next thirty-six years and will continue to double every thirty-six years thereafter. This same growth rate if it continues for 300 years would lead to a world population of one million millions. In the face of these figures it seems inevitable that any serious approach to the population problem must consider ways and means of checking this phenomenal growth rate. Yet the encyclical is silent on this point.

Thus in answer to the question posed at the beginning of this article as to how the encyclical fares when judged by the standards of contemporary discourse, one feels bound to admit that the verdict is not favourable. From a scientific standpoint, as we have seen, the discussion is inadequate at a number of points. While it is admitted that the encyclical contains many valuable things and in some ways makes a notable advance, nevertheless in the central issues it has failed to make its case. It is often asked in this connection 'What else could the Pope have said?' The answer to that is to be found in the theological report of his

own commission[4] – a document notable for its balancing of
the old and the new, of the demands of tradition and of progress
and for this reason likely to commend itself very favourably to
scientifically oriented men of good will.

4. This report is published in *On Human Life*, Burns Oates, London
1968.

J. P. MACKEY

TEACHING AUTHORITY IN FAITH AND MORALS

It is difficult to say who is responsible, or most responsible, for the present division in the Church over the birth-control issue, and perhaps it is futile at this stage to try to apportion the responsibility. All who love the Church must deeply regret the scandal of the division and must deeply regret also their own actions at least in so far as these can have contributed in any way to it. If we act on the assumption that all the responsibility is not on any one side, we may begin by asking what responsibility or amount of responsibility, not the hierarchy or the laity, but the theologians could now acknowledge. Of all the headings under which the theologians could now examine their consciences and either admit guilt or try to acquit themselves – that their dissent was too hasty, too public, too strongly phrased, and so on – there is one heading which is particularly central to the present situation and the examination of the theologians' conscience might well begin at this central point.

Is it not true that theologians have tarried too long over an analysis in depth of authority in the Church? Certainly, books and articles on this subject are increasing in number, since everybody nowadays at least pays lip-service to the view that we are in a crisis of authority in Church and world, but most of these works, if not all, have directed their attention to the exer-

cise of authority in the present situation of the Church, com-
paring or contrasting this with the biblical norms. In pursuance
of this totally worthy objective they have, however, for the
most part contrived to speak about the matter of authority, that
is, the subject matter concerning which authority is exercised,
without the necessary analysis into parts and kinds. The subject
matter of the Church's teaching authority is normally stated to
be revealed truth in two categories, namely, faith and morals.
The very fact that two categories are usually mentioned should
in itself warn theologians that an analysis into parts and kinds
is essential here, that at least one ought not to speak globally
of faith-and-morals as if one were dealing with one undifferen-
tiated whole.

The teaching issued by Church authority is of two kinds, not
simply by reason of its subject matter, as just now mentioned,
but also by reason of the degree of solemnity both of the
authority which issues the teaching and of the manner in which
the teaching is issued. The teaching is claimed to be infallible
when issued by the pope *ex cathedra* or by the united hierarchy
as a matter of faith or morals to be held by the whole Church.
Otherwise it is authoritative or authentic teaching, as it is sometimes called. Infallible teaching is characterized by the fact that,
as the First Vatican Council said, it is irreformable (Denz.
3074). Authoritative teaching, although as the Second Vatican
Council put it, it demands, certainly when issued by the pope, 'a
religious submission of mind and will' (*Lumen Gentium,* 25),
is admittedly reformable. (This non-infallible type of authoritative teaching, or authoritative teaching simply, is sometimes
referred to as authentic teaching. But perhaps the word 'authentic' smuggles in an impression that the teaching in question is
not only official, that is, adopted and presented by official
leaders in the Church, but also certainly correct, and thus not
really reformable. The English word does convey that impression and so may contribute to the further impression that
authoritative teaching is a lesser form of infallible teaching,
rather than teaching which is in quite a different category. This

in turn often leads to a kind of double-think whereby, on the one hand, we say that a teaching is not infallible and is therefore reformable but, on the other hand, we sometimes carry too far and too long our reluctance to actually admit the possibility of inadequacy or error in this teaching.)

Whatever one wants to make of that digression on titles and terminology, we have now two, superimposable, distinctions: between faith and morals, and between infallible and simply authoritative teaching. Our question, then, is this, can teaching be infallible or authoritative in the same way or to the same extent in the realm of faith and in the domain of morality? This is where analysis into parts and kinds comes in. The question will have to be answered separately for infallible teaching and for authoritative teaching, but since this chapter is being written in the context of the *Humanae Vitae* debate, and scarcely anyone would claim that document to contain an infallible pronouncement, much less space need be devoted here to infallible teaching than needs to be devoted to authoritative teaching.

There are some major differences between the realm of faith and the domain of morals. These differences must be stated and analysed in full consciousness of the organic unity that binds faith and morals, but they must be stated and analysed nonetheless. If the realm of faith is taken to include our acquaintance with the personal God as a result of his self-revelation to us and of the implications for our own existence and destiny of his very approach to man, moral demands of the highest order are made on man. This is clearly and consistently stated in the Bible and many of man's more detailed moral duties are accordingly spelled out for him. But unless we are never to write anything shorter than a book we can only say one thing at a time, and we must here dwell on the differences, not the organic unity, between faith and morals.

Faith and Morals

It has become commonplace in contemporary theology to say

that revelation was not a series of dictated propositions, but rather an event (in the case in which our interest lies it was the Christ-event) and the teaching in which the significance of this event was explained. It has similarly become commonplace to say that faith is not merely an intellectual assent to a set of propositions but rather a personal commitment to the God who revealed himself in Christ. Nevertheless, faith, like revelation before it, does have an intellectual or propositional side to it. We must be able to say who or what this God is to whom we claim to be personally committed, also what gives us grounds for this claim that we are or can be personally committed in this way, and what are the implications of this commitment. Teaching was part of the revelation event itself, and the attempt to formulate what we believe and why and to what effect is an essential part of our very commitment to God. It is this teaching part of the revelation and this continuing attempt at formulation together with the formulations that have resulted over the centuries that are meant here by the phrase 'the realm of faith'. The domain of morals again in this context is taken primarily to refer to the attempt to *say* what men ought to do: again propositions are in question, whether they take the form of commands or advice or any other form.

The realm of faith, then, is co-extensive with revelation. Whatever proposition we may put forward as a doctrine of the faith we mean to be taken as either a recasting or repetition of the teaching of Christ or a description of an aspect of the salvation-event which was his coming, his life, death, resurrection and present lordship. We realize that from the very earliest times men have not satisfied themselves, nor could they do so, with simple repetition of Christ's own words so that the propositional content of the faith would never change even in a single word. Christ himself took up the natural and traditional categories of thought of his contemporaries in order to explain his own significance for mankind, and, ever since, his followers have tried to understand him and his significance in the ever-changing natural and traditional categories in which each time and place can alone comprehend what is said to it. In short, the revelation is embodied in natural and traditional categories and this embodiment is a perennial task for the Church. The realm of faith, therefore, contains this natural or traditional element which, since these categories are constantly changing in content or in the impressions they convey, is itself constantly changing. We are familiar, then, with the phenomenon of development of dogma, however hard put we might be to explain the precise mechanics of this process. In any case, it is our hope, and our belief, that the original revealed truth should not in this inevitable process be taken from or added to or itself changed into something else. In the realm of faith we try to keep the whole truth and nothing but the whole truth of the original revelation, even if we do this by changing the expression of it.[1]

The first difference between the realm of faith and the domain of morality is this: although there is development in both areas (in the area of the faith this is called development of dogma), the development in the area of morality is far more substantial and involves far, far more of the purely rational ingredient. The reasons why this is so are many and complicated, but it is not difficult to hint at least at the main ones.

First, it is the work of another chapter to deal with the matter of the precise status of the main body of moral teaching in the Bible, in particular whether it can be taken to have been directly revealed by God or was gathered by the biblical writers from the cultures in which they lived or with which they were in contact, and if, in the latter case, they added anything to it or refined it in any way. Suffice it to say here for our immediate purposes that there is considerable evidence to the effect that a good deal of the moral teaching contained in the Bible was in fact gathered from the best of profane sources and is due, therefore, to reason rather than to revelation: that the main body of moral teaching attributed in the New Testament to Christ himself is of a rather peculiar nature; it is less an attempt to lay

1. I have dealt with this question more fully in *Tradition and Change in the Church*, Dublin and Sydney 1968.

down straightforward moral precepts (when he dealt with these
he assumed them from the Old Testament rather than create
ones of his own), than to illustrate and impress the ideal of
personal love.[2] Advice to pluck out an eye or give your coat
when your cloak is taken from you can scarcely be understood
as straightforward moral precept. Even from these few points it
would seem to follow that the domain of morals in Christian
teaching is not co-extensive with revelation, as was true in the
case of the realm of faith. Attempts to set out a code of moral
precepts cannot claim a complete basis in revelation, as can
attempts to set out a system of dogma, since it is not possible to
say that a complete code of moral precepts was revealed, or even
a set of moral principles from which such a code could simply
be deduced. The ideal of personal love, no matter how well
illustrated or accepted, does not make the content of our moral
duty clear to us automatically; only moral precepts can do this,
and even if we do not agree that the whole of our moral lives
should be governed by precept, that more positively proposed
values should also have their part, a basic code of precepts is the
backbone of any moral system, and it is difficult to show that
even such a code was revealed.

The general thesis at this point, namely, that the domain of
morals in Christian teaching is not co-extensive with revelation
as is the case with the realm of faith, is further reinforced by
everything that can be said of the mutability of moral law over
the centuries. Because of this element of mutability it would
simply not be possible to lay down for people of two thousand
years ago even a basic code of moral precepts that would still
be applicable today in the same form. It is true that we have
usually stressed the immutability of the moral law, arguing that
it is meant to perfect human nature and that does not change,
arguing also that it is in part the eternal plan of God for his
world and that does not change either, thereby ignoring the real
changes in the condition of man that an evolution-conscious
age can substantially document, and assuming that we know the

2. Cf. C. H. Dodd, *Gospel and Law*, Cambridge 1951.

eternal plan of God as it exists in his mind and that our precepts reflect this, which is precisely what is in question every time a precept is claimed to be a truly moral precept. Already in the thirteenth century Aquinas could point to the twin sources of change in the moral or natural law, namely, development or change in man's knowledge of it and change in the human situation, though he scarcely realized in his time the extent of that second source. For one thing, he was scarcely aware of the extent to which man himself changes that natural extension of himself which can be called the human situation, and thus really changes himself. Perhaps some future analysis of the mutability of moral law will unite these twin sources and see them more as a unitary factor: man's developing knowledge of his nature and his world changing successively his condition and his codes. There will never be question of denying the real immutability of the moral law in its essential framework and direction, but this will have to be shown to be, as in so many other matters, a question of permanence through development.

It would be out of line with the main purpose of this paper to spend too much time in discussing the nature and extent of mutability in the moral law, but since our normal prejudices run contrary to accepting such mutability to any substantial extent, let the following few points be made.

First, mutability is indicated in the very nature of moral judgements, and in this these judgements differ from propositions that belong to the realm of faith. Philosophers have long been accustomed to making a distinction between the speculative and the practical intellect, between theoretical and practical judgements. This distinction may have been expressed too strongly in the famous Humean dichotomy, then carried on in much of the British empirical tradition, between 'ought' and 'is', but it should at least have warned prospective analysts that they were dealing with two different types of judgement, so that ways of deciding truth, or permanent truth, might not at all be the same for both kinds. Clearly, if I make a theoretical or 'is' judgement, if I give H_2O as the formula for water, there will usually be some stable and objective structure against which my judgement will be checked. The propositions that belong to the realm of faith are of this nature; they are propositions that use the past or present or future tenses of the verb 'to be'; they are 'is' judgements.

But if I make an 'ought' judgement, I am making what is well called a value judgement, that is, I am talking about a value, an ideal, something which by definition is not and may not be actual, realized. Certainly in making moral judgements I must see to it that they accord with the essential structures of human nature, or the structures of the general human situation, as these are already given and to the extent that they are known, but from the nature of the case, being in accord with the given structures must mean something different here from what it means in the case of theoretical judgements. It must mean developing structures rather than reflecting them in accurate theory. And if a value judgement, by definition, cannot simply be one which reflects in accurate theory the essential structures of human nature, much less can it be regarded as a theoretical reflection of the given biological structures of the human organism with its irregularities, its correctable infertility and so on. Value judgements embody values, ideals, things not yet realized, and so they carry within themselves an indication of progress, development, change.

Then, if man does act as he feels he ought, since action is effective for better or worse, it alters the situation in which he finds himself, it changes his condition in the world and to that extent changes himself and his moral problems. So it is that, within the overall stability of the species, man and his morals are in continual evolution. Man, the moral agent, does not simply act in straightforward accordance with the literal theory of the given. On the contrary, in formulating ideals for himself and acting to realize these, he adapts himself and his environment in a creative mutual dependence on each other. Every realized value of his changes the objective situation, rather than literally reflecting it. This is notoriously obvious from the acceleration of his recent scientific advances. We do feel ourselves entitled to question the scientist about his responsibility for the progress, if such it is, which he makes when he invents a contraceptive pill, a fertility drug, or a method of nuclear fission, but we are even more obviously faced with a whole new set of moral problems once these advances have been made. Man's environment, his being in the world, to that extent his existential nature, has once more been irreparably changed. Clearly, a history of morals would illustrate this theme even more successfully, just as Noonan's book illustrates that contraception was not thought to be, and was not, the same thing over all the centuries during which the Church took its variously nuanced stand towards it.[3] Obviously these few remarks say more about mutability than they say about corresponding immutability, but then mutability is the neglected partner in our Catholic theory, and in any case they serve only to indicate a problem that is dealt with far more adequately elsewhere,[4] and simply to reinforce the main point at issue here, namely, that the realm of faith is co-extensive with revelation in a manner in which Christian moral teaching is not and could not be. Both in order to translate the ideal of personal love into at least a basic code of good conduct (though the ideal would never be exhausted in the fulfilment of any code) and in order to develop codes in step with the developing human situation, a very large ingredient of human reasoning is necessary which is not supplied for by revelation and cannot by any stretch of the imagination be regarded as a simple process of deduction from revealed premises.

Thirdly, and finally, not only is this ingredient of human reasoning made necessary in the domain of morals because of man's evolutionary situation, it is also made necessary by the very nature of the moral response itself. In order to act truly as a moral agent, in the full dignity of that state, man needs to be

3. J. T. Noonan, *Contraception: a History of its Treatment by Catholic Theologians and Canonists*, Harvard 1965.

4 See 'New Thinking on Natural Law', *Herder Correspondence*, December 1967.

able to know by his own reason whether what he contemplates doing is right or wrong. Only if he does something out of his own conviction, out of his own ability to reason and to see that it is a good thing, is his action a fully human moral action. Otherwise it is an act of obedience (acts of obedience are all moral actions, or at least may be, but not all moral actions should be acts of obedience, except perhaps in the case of young children), or a piece of pure conformity with little or no moral value. So, whereas an act of faith, by its very nature, is based on revelation and not on man's own powers of reasoning (though man may of course reason as to whether it is reasonable to accept an alleged revelation or not), for we can know the hidden God and his will towards man only on the strength of his revealing himself to us, a moral judgement, in order to be truly and fully such, must be based on reason; only in default of this on revelation, and then preferably on the kind of revelation that enables man himself to discover for himself that what he is asked to do is in fact the good thing to do.

Therefore, as any moral philosopher knows, there is a certain irreducible autonomy in the sphere of morality, basically an autonomy of the human reason, which is not to be found in the sphere of faith as such. Kant was the great exponent of this autonomy of morals and, however much we may disagree with other aspects of his philosophy, there can be no doubt about the fact that we Christians have for too long neglected, if not rejected, this his major moral insight. In a celebrated passage, Kant sums up the two latter points made in this section, namely, that there is no static ideal of human perfection (what he calls the ontological conception of perfection) which we possess in our minds or have revealed to us by God and from which we could simply draw a code of moral precepts for all time, and that, by the very nature of the moral life itself, we cannot be required to act in accordance with a moral code simply because someone says that it is the moral code, simply because someone reveals it. The passage is worth quoting in full, and certainly worth meditating on at length.

Amongst the rational principles of morality, the ontological conception of perfection, notwithstanding its defects, is better than the theological conception which derives morality from a divine, absolutely perfect will. The former, no doubt, is empty and indefinite, and consequently useless for finding in the boundless field of possible reality the greatest amount suitable for us; moreover, in attempting to distinguish specifically the reality of which we are now speaking from every other, it inevitably tends to turn into a circle, and cannot avoid tacitly presupposing the morality which it is to explain; it is nevertheless preferable to the theological view, first because we have no intuition of the divine perfection, and can only deduce it from our own conceptions, the most important of which is that of morality, and our explanation would thus be involved in a gross circle; and, in the next place, if we avoid this, the only notion of the divine will remaining to us is a conception made up of the attributes of desire for glory and dominion, combined with the awful conception of might and vengeance, and any system of morals erected on this foundation would be directly opposed to morality.[5]

Strong words, no doubt, but no one who cannot sustain the full brunt of them can claim to have a satisfactory moral theory.

Recta ratio, as even Aquinas could acknowledge, is the basic source of moral precepts, and *recta ratio* is human reason judging rightly. Judging what? Judging what man is in the concrete and ever-changing circumstances of his present world and, consequently, judging how best he may behave himself. Of course, if God were to issue specific moral precepts, the greatest possible presumption would run in favour of their being correct (this would be a presumption if man was unable to see the correctness of them for himself) and no man would be fool enough to disregard them. But again, as any moral philosopher

---

5. I Kant, *Fundamental Principles of the Metaphysics of Ethics* (E. tr. T. K. Abbott), London 1949, 74.

can point out, and most worthwhile moral philosophers do, such a presumption, namely, that a precept issued by God is in fact good, is itself based on man's knowledge that God is good, morally good that is. Naturally in order to know that God is good, man must have some prior (at least logically prior) knowledge of good and evil directly available to himself. Consequently, such precepts, if they ever were issued by God would, in principle at least, be open to investigation and verification by man, since it is impossible to have any knowledge of good and evil without possessing a criterion by which one can judge what is good and what is evil, and such a criterion has universal application once it is found and possessed. If the person revealing or issuing the precept is not God but one who claims to speak in the name of God, one who claims to exercise vicarious authority, then as J. M. Cameron has pointed out at some length,[6] we must have in our possession some criterion by which we can judge whether what he sets before us is good as we presume God would wish it to be. Otherwise we have no way of knowing whether this person is truly acting vicariously in this instance, and if we cannot *see* that an exercise of authority is truly an exercise of vicarious authority in a moral matter, then it is not an exercise of vicarious authority. It is of the essence of vicarious authority that it be seen to be exercised vicariously.

What is morally good is what is good for man, as all ethical theories, however they may designate themselves, admit. Man's final destiny, we believe, is not in his own hands, or entirely of his own making, and so his religious duties are not for him to discover. But grace is embodied in nature, which man does know and manipulate, and is not perfected apart from nature. Therefore, discovery and implementation of the best he can do and make of himself and of his world is man's contribution to the work of redemption and the source of his dignity as God's partner in the work.

One could sum up the argument of this section on the differ-

6. See his *Images of Authority*, London 1966.

ences between the realm of faith and the domain of morals as follows: it appears (a) from the probable source of most of even the biblical moral teaching, (b) from the development that can be expected, and seen, in moral codes over the centuries, and (c) from the very nature of a truly moral decision or action, that morality is based on reason, and must be based on reason, in a manner in which faith is not and cannot be; conversely, that the realm of faith is co-extensive with the content of special divine revelation in a manner in which the moral teaching of the Church is not, and that faith is totally dependent on the revelation event in a manner in which morality of its nature cannot be.

Infallibility

We ask, then, first, whether we can speak of the pope or the hierarchy, or even the whole Church, being infallible in matters of faith-and-morals, without even considering the possibility of there being a difference in the status of our statement or claim as we pass from faith to morals? This question is asked in view of the conclusion of the last section that Church moral teaching is not co-extensive with revealed truth in the manner in which its teaching of the faith is claimed to be.

In the actual wording of the definition of papal infallibility from the First Vatican Council the subject matter with respect to which this prerogative is exercised is simply stated to be 'doctrine regarding faith or morals' (Denz. 3074) and, although in the text leading up to this definition there is talk of Roman pontiffs defining 'those things which with the help of God they had recognized as conformable with the Sacred Scriptures and Apostolic Traditions', there is no definite statement to the effect that the exercise of infallibility is confined to the area of revealed truth. The belief that the prerogative of infallibility is operative only within the confines of revealed truth may be read into the Second Vatican Council's *Constitution on the Church*, especially where it is stated that: 'This infallibility with which our divine redeemer willed his Church to be endowed when she defines a doctrine of faith or morals, is co-extensive with the deposit of

divine revelation which must be religiously guarded and faith-
fully expounded' (par. 25); but it is difficult to say if it is as yet
clear and universal teaching. Certainly, the manuals on which
we were brought up were pretty well unanimous in holding that
the prerogative of infallibility was operative far outside the
range of revealed truth. They maintained that the Church could
be infallible with regard to certain truths of natural reasoning
which were essential as an outer defence of the doctrines of the
faith, and if they wavered a little about theological conclusions,
as they were called, that is, conclusions to syllogisms made up
of one revealed truth and one truth of natural discovery, they
were happy to extend the prerogative of infallibility to such
things as the canonization of saints.

As already stated, it is not our purpose here to go into this
question of infallibility at any length, since our present interest
centres mainly on authoritative teaching simply as such. Suffice
it to say, therefore, that perhaps the solution to the apparent
clash of views as between the Second Vatican Council and most
of the text-books, which in any case are all pre-conciliar, may
well lie in seeing that the division of different kinds of truths –
revealed, explicitly or implicitly, rational, theological conclusion, and so on – is a highly artificial one. The Christian tradition as a whole does not illustrate this kind of division of
truths taught. What does seem to happen, as already suggested,
is that the new salvation event is embodied in natural and traditional categories of understanding, and that, if one is infallible,
one is so with respect to this totality and not with respect to
artificially segregated parts of it. A suggestion which does seem
to be on the horizon, therefore, would read something like this:
that a claim to infallibility has varying strength and cogency as
we move out from the central and simply stated truths of the
Christian salvation event and embody these in more and more
of the ever-changing categories of natural thought and experience. A comparative study of the history of theology and the
history of authoritative teaching will quickly enough reveal how
little the teaching Church bound itself to particular theological

systems, how it always preferred the statement which was as close as possible to the content, if not the terminology, of the Scriptures. On the other hand, if the suggestion just made has any value in it, and if the conclusion of the last section is true, then claims to infallibility in the teaching of morals, especially in the laying down of moral rules, will be weakest and should be most tentative of all. This would seem to be the least conclusion that could be drawn by anyone who realizes what a substantial amount of purely rational material there is in Church moral teaching, and who is also convinced that infallibility is a prerogative that is operative only within the area of revealed truth. Furthermore, because of the development that is native to moral codes it is difficult to see how the character of being irreformable, which is the character of infallible teaching, can apply over the range of moral teaching.

The important question at this time, however, concerns something less than infallible teaching. If infallibility were claimed for the recent declarations on birth-control (as it is not and perhaps if it were, then, in accordance with what has been said above, the claim might have to be a much diluted one), the declarations could be accorded the authority of truth itself, though at a second remove. This means that it would not be the authority of truth itself which is borne in on us by its own evidence, but the authority of a statement which is known to be true by means of another truth, namely, that the Spirit of God preserved the Church from error in this matter.

Authoritative Teaching

We are here concerned with something less than infallibility. Our question precisely is, what is this thing and how does it function or, rather, how should it function in particular in the realm of moral legislation? Perhaps it would be better to leave aside the question, how does it actually function? It is very likely that that question would take us too far afield again in the direction of a critique of actual practice. For instance, when we admit, as we do of course always admit, that a non-infallible statement is reformable, we might have to ask, who actually reforms these statements when they are in fact reformed? And we might find it difficult to point to many actual instances when the hierarchy or its offices took the initiative. If we then said that it is the theologians, for instance, who often have taken the initiative in attempting the reform of such admittedly reformable teaching (and that they normally have done this and have felt, rightly or wrongly, that they had to do it, not in the way that the text-books recommend, namely, by making their objections privately known to Rome), we must come up against another very practical problem. How long must they wait before expressing their dissent? Here again the length of time has probably varied in practice according to the nature of the subject and the amount of work already done on it, and there can scarcely be a settled and precise norm to govern every case.

Strictly speaking, where the teaching of truth is concerned there should be no question of authority at all; the truth should recommend itself by its own intrinsic evidence. But this ideal situation is never realized in fact, for if we were to wait for all the necessary truths by which we live to impress themselves on us by their own intrinsic evidence, the business of living simply could not go on.

Authority, then, first in our experience attaches to certain persons. We automatically follow and respect men whom we know to habitually speak the truth and to preach and practise what is right. On the other hand, we insist that all authority ceases when a man in whatever position, teaches what is in fact untrue or immoral. Obviously, however, we cannot all of us check, nor can any one of us check in every instance, the truth or rightness of all the rules and beliefs which are put before us to inspire our lives and to guide our action. So we are here already at the first level of practical presumption: certain people exercise authority over us because we presume, on the record of the good we know them to have done and the truth we know them to have spoken, that they do habitually teach what is true and good. Where this possibility of checking is concerned, there is a difference once again between the realm of faith and the domain of morals. In the case of articles of faith, though some kind of checking with an authoritative source such as the Bible is in principle possible, the role of Church tradition, which gave rise to the Bible itself, is such that we must finally accept the veracity of privileged witnesses and we simply cannot test everything at the court of direct evidence. In the case of moral precepts this kind of checking is always in principle possible. That it is not always a practical possibility for many people and in many instances gives rise to the first level of practical presumption.

Then, because this level of practical presumption is a general feature of human society, some people are specially commissioned, by men or by God, to teach a true philosophy of life and to see it implemented. This is their special task in life, given them as a result of their special competence or special privileges. It is their particular service to their fellow men. Methods of selection and appointment vary in society, naturally, and so there is added at this point a second level of practical presumption, the presumption, namely, that the men who are set in positions of responsibility in any society are set there by reason of their real competence, their record for truth and rightness, and not for any less worthy reasons. The Church, being a community, would naturally have evolved such leadership structures if they had not been given it specifically by its founder. Luckily, though, leadership structures were given the Church by Christ himself. Luckily, because he also gave clear instructions as to how these structures were to be exercised. The main instruction may have been negative – 'You know that among the pagans the rulers lord it over them, and their great men make their authority felt. This is not to happen among you' (*Matt.* 20:25) – but not the less important for that.

Because it is not possible for everyone in society to check the truth of every rule and belief proposed to him for himself, or to check the motives of the leaders or of those who put them in power, then, for the sake of order, stability and progress in the community, the presumption runs at the two levels mentioned that what the duly constituted leaders do and say is right. On the basis of the positions these have been given, on the basis of these presumptions, the more legal type of authority in society comes into being, that is, the authority of the *ipse dixit*, the authority of a teaching or measure that stems from the position of the one who adopted it officially. The need for such leaders in any community and the presumptions that run in their favour, these form the connecting link between the two extreme types of authority – the basic authority of truth or rightness that impresses us by its own evidence, and the authority that accrues to a measure from the simple fact that it is officially adopted – so that one can be seen to flow from the other. We do, then, recognize that when, but only when, there is considerable evidence, after the most careful checking, that a stand taken by leaders is not, or not completely, true or right, we may question the legal type of authority in favour of the more basic authority of the truth itself. In the rest of this chapter we shall be dealing with the authority of persons or offices, with authority in its more legal form, especially with its nature and role in properly moral matters.

Just as infallibility was formerly stated to be applicable to faith and morals with scarcely any attempt to distinguish the extent or mode of its application in these two rather different spheres, so also was hierarchical authority. But here again, in the case of hierarchical authoritative teaching no less than in the case of infallible teaching, distinctions must be made in the extent and mode of its application in two different spheres. The self-revelation of God, together with its implications for man, is simply not available to scientific or philosophical research (as indeed is true of even human self-revelation) – if it were, it would not be self-revelation. So, if it is made at a particular place and point of time, it must be carried on in the tradition of a community. Although, as has been said already, a certain limited amount of checking with old and authoritative documents is possible here, nevertheless, the constituted leaders of the community, whose special task it is to preserve the tradition in its purity, must see the presumption of their competence, the presumption of the correctness of what they say, in short, the presumptions on which the more legal type of authority is founded, run in their favour in the realm of faith to the fullest possible extent.

One has only to remember the substantial part that human reasoning played and must continue to play in the evolution of moral codes, one has only to remember the necessity of reasoning to one's own moral convictions, the necessity of understanding one's moral positions by the light of one's own reason if one would be truly a moral agent, one has only to remember these things in order to see that the legal type of authority cannot at all be given the same place in morals as it can be allowed in the realm of faith. It can be seen, then, that an appeal to authority, to an *ipse dixit*, to a will human or divine, making some action good or evil, may be quite contrary to the very nature of morality itself. Man the moral agent, and every man who wishes to act truly as a moral agent, must have some independent way of knowing that the legislator or teacher of morality is laying down good moral precepts. He must possess some idea of the moral criterion and so be in principle capable of testing for himself the moral precept proposed to him. Only in so far as he acts out of personal appreciation of the truth or rightness of the precept is he truly a moral agent at all.

Needless to say, none of this denies the necessity for authorities in society who will have charge of moral teaching also and in whose favour will run, for the sake of goodness and order, the presumption that what they say is right. But all this does have very important implications for the manner in which authorities teach morals in society, and for the manner in which their teaching must be regarded by their subordinates. For instance, it is seen to be essential that the authorities act as guides showing the way to the realization of better and better moral values in concrete circumstances of the time and place – showing this *so that it can be seen by others* – not as legislators giving the impression that something is right or wrong because they said so. They simply cannot act authoritatively here in the same way or to the same extent that they could act authoritatively in the case of truths of the faith which are preserved only in the tradition of the community, or, to take quite a different example, in the way and to the extent that they could act authoritatively in matters of purely positive law of the society which they govern. If they did they would be acting against the very nature of morality. They surely must show reason for their suggested moral precepts, must guide the reason of the individual so that he can act truly rationally, truly morally, rather than supplant it so that he is at best simply obedient as the subject of a given authority and at worst a conformist and not really a moral agent at all.

The conclusion to this argument is a conclusion which is illustrated by the constant practice of even the most elementary texts in moral philosophy and theology, if it is not constantly reiterated in them. It is this: the reasoning in a moral text which comes before a moral conclusion or precept stands in the most intimate possible relationship to that latter, so much so that if the reasoning is seriously impugned by a sufficient number of competent and responsible people (whether these be theorists mainly or mainly drawing their insights from the practice of daily life) the conclusion, the moral precept, must also be considered seriously impugned, as must also be the authority, in this instance at least, of the one who laid down this law. There seems to be no way of shirking that fact.

Certainly, the Church is under the guidance of the Spirit of God and certainly the hierarchy can claim to receive special guidance from the Spirit of God, and the Church as a whole has, in its search for moral values, the example and the inspiration of the finest love that the world has ever known; but love will guide, without in the least supplanting reason or making up for serious lacunae in it, in the attempt to lay down moral precepts (and it is such 'propositions' that are in question here when morality is mentioned), and the guidance of the Spirit of

God also must surely be thought to operate in this area according to the nature of the subject matter. First and most obviously, this guidance is never claimed to amount to new revelation; hence if someone says that moral laws (presumably the existing moral code of laws is that in question) are immutable because God's law is immutable, he is either making a very strong claim or hiding a very large presupposition. He is either claiming that man has some direct access to the mind of God on this particular matter, which could only be through divine revelation granted, or else he is presupposing that a precept at which man has arrived by the use of his finite reason on the complex and changing data of human nature in its concrete situation certainly reflects the will or law of God, but this is precisely what may be in question at certain stages in the moral progress of any society. In actual fact, at least in many cases, if not in all, man first tries to decide whether a particular moral precept is right or not and then knows it to be the law of God or not. The guidance of the Spirit in this area, therefore, must surely be thought to take the form of guiding men towards a fuller embodiment and expression of their relationship with God in the appreciation and perfection of their natural capacities, so that the guidance must be thought to at least partly take the form of guiding the reasoning, the natural intuition, by which these natural structures are actually known and their better fulfilment actually discovered. In short, the claim to the guidance of the Spirit, since it is not thought to include any new revelation, does not rule out of court the role of reason in morals and the consequent possibility of a rational check on suggested moral precepts.

In order to soften this conclusion, if softening it needs, it might be added that a rational critique of a suggested moral precept does not necessarily have to arrive at a simple and clear-cut decision that it is right, or the equally simple and clear-cut decision that it is wrong. Anyone familiar with the operations of reason will realize that, whether in processes of construction or criticism, it reaches conclusions with varying degrees of definiteness or finality. Criticisms of an absolutely imposed precept need not say that it does not contain a positive value as its main inspiration, but they may say that they just cannot see how it can be stringently imposed in that way in all circumstances. Similarly, on the constructive side, there are surely more ways than one in which to give expression to a moral insight. Not all moral precepts need, or probably could, be expressed in terms of absolute prohibition. Even the very basic precept 'thou shalt not kill' seems to need a very great deal of qualification, and yet there can be very few cases where, because of the seriousness of the matter, an absolute prohibition could be more reasonably expected. Moral insights can also be expressed in terms of values or ideals which are of obligation on every man to strive towards them but perhaps not of immediate obligation on some to realize, or to realize in the particular way suggested, for whom the attempt to do this in their present circumstances would involve too much damage to themselves or to others. There may be best and better ways of doing things, and these may change with circumstances, instead of there always being just right and wrong ways. If we took seriously the role of reason in morals we might easily reach conclusions such as these.

Conclusion

In conclusion, then, it is wrong, because it is contrary to the very essence of morality, to even seem to make something right or wrong by decree. The recent papal encyclical *Humanae Vitae* need certainly not be thought to have done this, even though some of its defenders did contrive to give the impression that that is what it did. The teaching of the encyclical obviously relied heavily on the reasoning given in it, and that reasoning is therefore relevant to an assessment of the authority behind the conclusion, relevant even to the claim that some light or guidance from supernatural sources was operative in this particular instance. Reason is too important in moral matters to be supplanted or have its serious lacunae, if such there are, glossed over.

The most basic authority of all is the authority of the truth that appeals to us by its own inherent attraction. In the search for the truth in the area of specific moral propositions or precepts human reasoning plays a major role. Purely legal authority, the *ipse dixit* of a man in virtue of the office he holds, has therefore in this area a more restricted function than it has in almost any other area. If that is true of legal authority when it functions in laying down moral precepts, it is even more true of that extension of legal authority which is called coercive authority. Hence, if the lines of argument in this article are at all acceptable, those who coerce by actual or threatened punishment must seriously ask themselves the question if even the desire, laudable in itself, to see to it that the whole community speak with one voice is any justification for such action, which is so hostile to the true nature of a truly moral response, especially in cases where the moral reasoning is not above suspicion.

It may be necessary to point out that the point being made here has to do with the objective forum of moral truth or falsehood, adequacy or inadequacy, not with the internal forum of conscience. Conscience has its inalienable rights whether its judgement is correct or not, rights that are limited, of course, as all human rights are. What is to be feared in moral debate is this: that talk about the rights of the individual conscience might be so used as to obscure issues of objective evidence for moral conclusions. People who extol the rights of the individual conscience in the course of any particular moral controversy should be made to explain exactly what they mean. Do they mean that an official decision is correct in their view, that those who disagree are therefore definitely erroneous, but have the rights of the *erroneous* conscience? Or, are they not prepared to say unambiguously that the official decision is correct, so that their talk about the freedom of the individual conscience can convey the impression not only that people may disagree, but that there is, in their view, a possibility that in disagreeing these people might even be correct? Unless people who extol the rights of the individual conscience in the course of moral controversy explain exactly where they stand themselves, by answering these questions, then they are bound to be suspected of using the conscience issue as a smoke-screen, of not wanting to agree fully with the official decision while at the same time not wanting to say this clearly. Therefore, it is necessary to say quite clearly that in this paper we are concerned to say that reasoning is intimately bound to moral conclusions so that, objectively and without reference to the rights of the individual conscience even when it is in error, defects in reasoning shown up perhaps by serious and sustained challenges to it, should not be easily made up for by the exercise of legal authority in its purer forms. That would only make for obedience with little or no understanding in it, and that is not a moral virtue of very high standing; or for conformity, and that is not a virtue at all.

In short, it has been the aim of this paper to prick the theological conscience at one particular point. Theologians have spoken of infallibility and of authority in the Church 'in matters of faith and morals'. The question is put, is it right to speak so without distinctions? It is then suggested, as a matter for much further thought and research, that the meaning and role of authority, just as the meaning and role of infallibility (though not in the same way), must be made more precise, depending on whether we are speaking about the realm of faith or the domain of morals; that global and indistinct statements embracing both prerogatives and both areas are unworthy of any truly accurate theological thinking.

ENDA MCDONAGH

THE THEOLOGY OF CONSCIENCE

It might appear that recent advances in various departments of theology, in particular the Council statement on religious liberty, had contributed to a new understanding of the role of conscience in the Christian life. This is not so. The debate has now been focused with the encyclical *Humanae Vitae,* but it could be maintained that no real advance has been made in the theology of conscience for many centuries.

The theological presuppositions of conscience are easy. If God has spoken to man asking for man's knowing and free response, then man must be capable of recognizing this personally and responding to it out of himself. This is presupposed in the whole of the Old Testament. We may not find the term or a worked out notion of conscience, but we do find the reality, and the term used – heart – is that taken up again in the New Testament in the Synoptics. It is with St Paul that both the word and the developed notion of the reality come to us in a fairly clearcut form: conscience is that which enables us to judge good and evil, that which reproaches us when we have done wrong, gives us a sense of contentment or peace when we have done well. It can make mistakes; we must respect the conscience of others. These are well known elements in the theology of conscience as we find them in St Paul, they are developed in a fragmentary way through the Fathers, taken up in a more systematic way by the Scholastics. With St Thomas the distinction between habitual and actual conscience, that is the general capacity to make moral judgements, and the practical immediate moral judgement about what one should or should not do, about what one has done, emerges in a systematic way.

Since that time, however, no very great advance has been made in the theology of conscience. Of course there was clarification and refinement, particularly in the controversies about a doubtful conscience. But it is debatable if this whole controversy contributed very much really to a deeper understanding of what conscience may mean.

This essay will examine some aspects of the theology of conscience which are in need of rethinking and development, but it could not hope to present a comprehensive and fully developed theology.

Conscience has for too long, almost since the time of the Scholastics, been given a very narrowly intellectualist interpretation. This interpretation has recently been questioned, to some extent corrected, and we have now a better idea of conscience as a judgement involving the whole person and not just an intellectual event. The whole person, emotional as well as intellectual, loving or committed as well as knowing, is involved in assessment of moral realities – moral realities involving a general pattern for life and particular activities. It is not enough to make an intellectual judgement; it must be a personal judgement. The sharp distinction, then, between on the one hand intellect and will and on the other hand intelligence and emotions, has perhaps blinded us at once to the complexity of conscience judgements and to their richness and possibilities. The interplay which goes on in a moral judgement between intelligence, emotion and will demands a good deal more careful study.

An honest conscience judgement demands openness to the full truth of the situation. Openness to the full truth of the situation is a matter of decision, not something that is already given, so that presupposed in every conscience judgement is some decision or commitment. This presupposition is not a question simply of unconscious forces, of inherited prejudices: it is the way a person gradually shapes his life, how he approaches reality, how, above all, he approaches other people. In his openness to reality and to the truth, he has to be constantly overcoming the tendency to tailor reality to his own needs and desires, his own presuppositions and prejudices, his own satisfactions. There is therefore in a conscience judgement this presupposition that one is willing to seek the full truth and to give oneself to it. It is a presupposition which may not be lightly taken for granted.

The personal commitment to the truth which is presupposed in a properly formed conscience judgement is affected by the person's temperament, his emotional condition both long-term and immediate. Somebody deeply disturbed emotionally is unlikely to reach a balanced judgement. On the other hand, emotional energy can be a powerful support in personal commitment and the effort demanded in seeking the truth. Indeed without some emotional energy, integrated, harmonized with, and at the service of his choice or commitment, a person will more easily give up the search. And his first awareness as well as his growing commitment may have emotional roots. The interplay between intellect, will and emotion has enormous influence in the final judgement and needs to be properly understood if that judgement is to be as true to reality as possible.

How commitment to the truth, presupposed as the conscience judgement, takes concrete shape differs from person to person of course. For the Christian it takes on a particular form, the form, as it were, of the incarnation. He sees as the ultimate truth God who has given himself in the person of his Son, who therefore asks for our response as sons of the Father and brothers of one another. This commitment to sonship and brotherhood and to acting, behaving as sons and brothers, commits us to discovering how a son or brother in the light of Christian revelation will behave in this situation. And this is where perhaps most of us fail: not that we do not act on our certain conscience judgements but that we are unwilling to pursue the implications of the situation we are in, unwilling to face up to the demands that may be made on us if we try to understand the situation fully. It is the failure to seek the truth at all costs and so have a properly informed conscience that is most common.

Conscience then involves a commitment to the truth, to seeking for the truth, which is totally personal; it has decision and emotional elements, as well as intellectual elements. And the harmony of these is necessary to the proper understanding of the conscience judgement.

The second difficulty which has perhaps inhibited a development of the theology of conscience is the form in which morality has been presented: a legal form, that is, and extrinsically. The difficulty about this model or form of morality is not that it is invalid at every or any level. Of course it has validity at a certain level, but only a secondary or derivative level. This is clear from the gospels and from Jesus's own criticism of the legalism and extrinsicism of the Pharisees; it ought to be clear too from the 'natural law' tradition that morality is something internal and inherent and should be primarily expressed in some form other than the legal. It is in fact a response to the deepest reality that is in man and the formulation of this in legal prescriptions or prohibitions is secondary, derived and always approximate. When the morality is presented in the legal form it comes as it were from outside; we attempt then to understand the law and to follow it, much as we attempt to understand human law and to follow it. This creates a false dilemma which is to be solved, according to the suggestion of some, by the interiorization of the law. This seems quite the reverse of what ought to happen. What we are looking for in formulations, and formulations we need, is not something we can interiorize; what we are looking for is an exterior expression of the internal reality that is there. Given a legal model of morality, however, we are inevitably faced with the problem of a law which is imposed on us from the outside and which, therefore, however much we may try to interiorize it, remains foreign to us; in obeying it we may be developing our capacity for obedience, we may be performing what is socially useful, we may in fact be respecting in some sense the rights of others, but we are not acting morally in the full sense. Why?

Because acting morally in the full sense is responding out of oneself to a challenge or invitation internal to self, written on the heart. The source of the challenge is God or the neighbour; the goal of it is self-transcendence to union with God and neighbour, but it arises within the self and demands a response from within. Moral development in any particular area is the actualizing from within of the capacity to respond to God and neighbour. In the area of verbal communication, truthfulness is the virtue which describes how in this area of communication with others we respond to them and develop ourselves as truthful beings, how we respect God and the neighbour in this area and so, moving out to them, expand and grow ourselves. The formula 'you must not lie', or even positively 'you must tell the truth in all circumstances', is a legal one which is extrinsic and does not involve understanding the internal relationship which binds one to God and the neighbour and which calls for this particular response. We must understand then the situation in which we are and how verbal communication expresses our relationship to God and the neighbour. The same applies to sexual communication, to respect for life, to the handling and control of material goods. In any area we must have an internal understanding of the value that is to be realized and then we can realize it as part of our true response to the other and a genuine development of ourselves. Otherwise we can go through the motions of obeying the law without really having respect for the other, having genuine love for him, expressing our brotherhood, and without co-relatively developing ourselves. We can tell the literal truth or we can go through the proper motions of sexual expression, but it is only from an internal understanding of how these express our true relationship to the other that we do in fact properly respect and love him and so genuinely develop ourselves.

It is not possible, therefore, to impose, as it were from the outside, moral directives which must be obeyed, to demand simply obedience and to regard obedience as morally developing in this area, for the person or indeed for the community. It is not responding to the other out of the person's internal reality but obeying an external directive. It is only in so far as he understands this directive as derived from the relationship he enjoys and the situation in which this relationship now makes a claim, it is only in so far as he understands this as internal to him, as coming from within the situation and from himself internally, that he can respond in a truly human and so in a truly Christian way.

The person, in his response in the situation in which he is, seeks to know the truth, the truth of the claim upon him; this is already part of his response, seeking to know the full truth of the claim upon him. If we take away this possibility of his internally understanding the truth of the claim upon him, we take away the possibility of his actually doing the truth. We take away the first stage of his response. If, therefore, we make detailed prescriptions externally for him in this way, and as it were enforce them in legal form, and consider the man virtuous who simply obeys them, we are distorting the notion of virtue, human response, human development. We are taking away the first step any man must make in any situation as a son of the Father and a brother of his fellow men. The conscience judgement is already part of the response: to have it made by somebody else removes the personal foundation for further response.

This is not to say that the individual is the creator of his own morality. He is not the creator, but he must be the knower, he must understand himself, what is demanded of him. This understanding, of course, is not something that comes to him by way of divine inspiration or by his own efforts alone: none of us understands anything as individuals. Whether it is mathematics or geography or philosophy, or morality, we are, as personal beings, members of and dependent upon the community. We can only understand and learn in community. This is the third aspect of the theology of conscience which needs development, because we have had no thorough-going examination of the relation between person and community, within our theology. Perhaps we haven't had it in philosophy either. Perhaps we shall always be inadequately equipped to understand the interchange between person and community. We can say on the one hand that the person is, to begin with, the product of some community that he is dependent on it for the colour of his hair as well as the accent of his voice. That it is from the community he gets his language as well as his food. That it is in a community that he grows and develops, psychologically, physically, and also morally. That what is available to him so that he can understand his moral situation, the relationships in which he is involved with God and the neighbour, the complex meaning of these relationships and the demands they imply, all this is given to him in the community. Out of all this he achieves some personal synthesis gradually and slowly and painfully; a synthesis that from time to time breaks down as new elements, new discoveries have to be integrated, new situations have to be faced, so that he reshapes his synthesis, his way of looking at life and out of this makes his further immediate and concrete decisions. This is a process that goes on whether we admit it or not, a process that goes on through the different communities to which we belong, so that they all have a role to play.

The person who would reject any form of community influence in his moral ideas and take his stand simply as an individual before God is deluding himself. He is ignoring the realities of the situation; he may reject for instance the official Church, but he belongs no less to other 'moral' communities. He inherits and accepts other moral ideas which are influencing him. There are other moral authorities operating on him, perhaps all the more effectively and all the more destructively because he is unaware of them. Private judgement in the popular sense is not only theoretically untenable but practically impossible. We are all shaped by the different overlapping communities in which we live – civil and ecclesiastical, voluntary and necessary. So that our moral ideas are not simply our own, and our moral decisions are not based on inspiration, human or divine; they are the personal attempt to use the elements of moral understanding of our varying communities which have grown and developed through history in order to understand as well as possible the claims made upon us and respond according to our understanding.[1]

In this situation it is clear that the Christian community of the Church has a role to play. It is not always obvious how that role is best fulfilled, or what the relationship is between the community and the individual Christian in regard to moral decision. It is clear that the Christian community, aware of man's call, aware of the gift of sonship, of saving sonship and brotherhood, has always understood it as involving a way of life in response. And that way of life has been understood, in its broad outline, at any rate, with great consistency and continuity by the Judaeo-Christian community moving through the Old Testament to the climax of the appearance of the Son of God in Jesus Christ. We have in the New Testament itself many obvious insights into how sonship and brotherhood should be lived in the world in which we are. Many of these are given very concretely as illustrations rather than as formal moral directives, but there is a shape of life there, a general shape of life which perhaps is not so original and unique in so far as its material moral demands are concerned, but as integrated into this picture of sonship and brotherhood it enables us to realize how at that time in that culture sonship and brotherhood had to be lived. In continuity with that time and that culture much of what was said there remains normative in our time because of our continuity, while some, because of discontinuity, is no longer appropriate, for example, St Paul on slavery.

1. Cf. E. McDonagh, 'The Christian Ethic: A Community Ethic', *Theology of Renewal II*, Montreal 1968.

Our continuity with that time enables us to see how the call to brotherhood and sonship can be or should be realized in many areas of life, at least in its general outline. But it is as you come down to detail that the cultural change makes a difference, and not only the cultural change but the personal vocation. As St Thomas pointed out the more concrete and determined one gets in moral prescription, the less general or universal is the application. However, the person is dependent on the historical community for his understanding of the basic Christian call and the general shape of how this call ought to be lived. The general Christian moral insights, which are, by and large, human insights because the call to sonship has to be lived in and through our humanity, remain valid for all. The particular shape and form they take on may vary. In regard to respect for life, this is fairly obvious. In regard to war, in regard to the use of material goods, much development has taken place. In regard to verbal communication, the problem of advertising for instance is a wholly new one, demanding new development of the morality of verbal communication. So that the development, the historical development, that is necessary must be taken into account.

Within this general structure and its historical development, the personal vocation remains no less real. Man is no less personal and ultimately unique because he belongs and must belong to a community. The community is only really a community in so far as it is composed of unique if interdependent persons. It is their very uniqueness which enables the community to be alive, to remain viable, open to development, to new life. Otherwise it degenerates into some kind of stagnant collectivity or ant heap. There is then a unique vocation for each within the community, a unique vocation which does not allow one to reject, still less, of course, to destroy the community, to ignore its moral insights on which we are all dependent, but which demands that we make our personal synthesis within the community. In our unique situation we shall be called to make our unique personal response which will fully respect the general insights handed on by the community but will integrate them in new and personal ways.

To take this a stage further and see how within the community this teaching should be formulated and presented to the people is an even more difficult problem. The Christian community has structures whereby the community understanding is articulated and developed; whereby judgement is made on whether a particular understanding or development is in line, in continuity with, the original Christian vision, or is departing from it. But again when it comes to moral realities this remains at a rather general level. No less demanding for that, no less true, no less verified in the situations in which we find ourselves; the general and constituent features or values of these situations where human beings attempt to live as sons of the Father and brothers of one another remain true. But how they are to be realized, incarnated in a particular person's life, depends on his understanding and his capacity for response.

It would appear then that the business of the community structures is to define in a rather general way what are the basic values to be realized in Christian living. Then at any particular time and in any particular situation the community must endeavour to understand how these values are to be realized, and must, above all, draw attention to areas where they are being ignored, where they are being degraded. There have been obvious examples of this recently in regard to war, in regard to racial and other discrimination. It is the business then of the community to come alive to particular positive demands that may be made upon it, to particular abuses that exist, and once it has examined and understood the situation, to speak out for these demands or against these abuses. Speaking out for particular demands or against particular abuses here and now is necessary if the Christian community is to remain credible, as a group called to show the way, to show how to live as sons of the Father and brothers of one another. But it should be remembered that there is a certain relativity about this speaking out, that it does apply to this situation here and now which has perhaps, long historical roots and is not going to be changed immediately; but we don't look for absolute moral judgements on these particular things – absolute in the sense of unchangeable and immutable. These are to some extent applications – applications of basic Christian and human insights.

If one condemns racial discrimination or slavery in the way St Paul didn't see fit or necessary, the particular application for the person living in a particular area can vary enormously with his own situation, family, business, capacity to endure various privations, opportunity for helping people, and so on. The obligation of the mayor of a city with racial problems will differ somewhat from the obligation of a citizen living in a slum area. The obligation of the well-fed citizen in the prosperous, white suburb will be different from that of the barely out-of-the-slum citizen fearful of falling back again if particular people move into his area, and so on. These are the types of problems which do not invalidate a general condemnation of discrimination as opposed to brotherhood in Jesus Christ, but make it more difficult to apply. This can only be done by the person in his situation.

There are at least three levels of moral understanding: the general structures in which brotherhood and sonship are expressed; the historical applications of these general structures in particular societies at particular times; and finally the personal vocation to realize the universal structures and the more particular applications in each person's life and behaviour. For this final stage in understanding, for the final living out of it, nobody can substitute, although many can help.

If a person is to live a fully human and Christian life, morality must be presented to him as an understanding of how as a son of the Father and brother of mankind he is to live, but this presentation outlining the general structures with more particular applications, cannot replace his final decision about how these elements are integrated in his personal situation.[2]

---

[2] An attempt to deal with this problem has been made by Karl Rahner in his distinction between 'essential' and 'existential' ethics.

A fuller theology of conscience as the Christian's understanding of his personal call within the community to respond to a particular moral demand, demands much more research and reflection on the three aspects outlined above. The interrelation of intelligence, emotion and will in conscience judgements, is a philosophical and psychological problem as well as a theological one. The character of the conscience judgement as an essential and primary step in man's response to God and not just a mechanical reading of the 'maker's instructions' suggests a new and non-legal approach to morality. And here it may be asked how far the emergence of a separate tract on conscience in the manual tradition parallel to the tract on law, has aggravated the difficulties of the relationship between objective and subjective morality, between authority and conscience. In a different presentation of morality, personal understanding might fit more easily into place without the same danger to 'objectivity' or 'personality'. There will remain, however, the need to analyse more closely the general relationship between person and community as far as personal understanding is concerned and to see how it is realized in the Christian community and in particular on moral issues. It may be possible to arrive at more satisfactory conclusions on these three aspects of the problem along the lines suggested in this essay.

PAUL SURLIS

THE CHURCH'S MESSAGE

Introduction

The aims of this chapter may be simply stated: they are to present some positive reflections on aspects of the role which the Church plays in assisting man to achieve the morally good life in the modern world. The method to be followed will consist largely in examining the documents of Vatican II to see what the Church in Council has said of her own role in teaching and forming modern man. It would be to misunderstand the function of the Council and its real achievement if we were to look to it for a complete and detailed treatment of any of the major topics which it discussed: much less should we look for such treatment of the present subject which deals with the entire field of life and religion. Likewise, complete and detailed treatment of the topic selected is not to be expected here. At most all that is offered are suggestions which would require detailed and comprehensive treatment later.

One of the principal tasks which the Church always faces is not merely to preach about morals but to create a society in which morality is possible. This is just another way of speaking about making life more human. It is the burden of the Church's message to modern man that the universal brotherhood which he seeks and from which he seems to be so far is not entirely a matter of human achievement, it is, in fact, grace or gift as well. The Church tells the modern world that the brotherhood of man is founded on the fatherhood of God: that not only is mankind one in origin and destiny, but also that mankind is one in Christ and that human life and not, therefore, explicitly Christian life, can become authentic and truly personal at the individual and community levels, only if what Christ is doing for men through his Spirit is recognized and only if men heed the summons to participate freely in this work.

The Church offers to man not only a message but a message of salvation which, far from negating or destroying human effort, values and aspirations, rather includes, perfects and transcends them. This message of salvation is founded on sacrifice, the sacrifice of God himself which means that 'God has endured men and Christians and that Jesus Christ has taken from them all their weaknesses, injustices, self-righteousness, malice and depravity and taken them upon himself and taken them down into his grave. His sacrifice means that to the deadly sins which are certainly no illusion, but secretly or openly, brutally or unnoticed, lay waste the goodness of creation daily and hourly, he offered his body and soul in order to bear them and to give us his life thereby. His sacrifice means that at least once in this world no claim was raised in reply to opposing claims but Jesus Christ offered his life in unconditional love as the indestructible and unconquerable foundation, as a foundation superior to death, as the resurrection of Jesus Christ from the dead proves.'[1] When subsequently we refer to the paschal mystery, or to the Church as the sacrament of unity and salvation for the whole human race we have this understanding of the meaning and value of Christ's work of salvation in mind. The Church's message to the man of today is found not in one document nor in the development of one theme from the Council. It is found in the total life, practice, preaching and worship of the Church. And it concerns the

1. Heinrich Schlier, *The Relevance of the New Testament*, London 1968, 129.

whole life of man, not in the sense of offering him a blueprint for every act and a solution for every problem, but in the sense of demanding from him in the concrete realities of daily living and in all his contacts with others freedom from self-preoccupation and anxiety and instead the discerning self-dedication – even to the point of sacrificing himself – to others which is called 'love of the neighbour'. This love is a possibility for man only because God has first loved him (cf. 1 *John* 4:19) and by his grace enables man to love in this way. In effect, the Church says to man today, 'Realize your true nature and your dignity', and the value of the Church's message lies in the fact that she has privileged information concerning God, man, Christ, and their relationships. The Church is the visible, audible, tangible expression of Christ, as Christ was of God and she exists to achieve faith, hope and charity in the hearts of men and thereby to give glory to God as Christ did.

Properly to treat of the role of the Church in achieving good moral living today would involve treating all these themes (and many others) in depth. While we cannot provide that comprehensive treatment here we can indicate, from the official documents of the Council, the lines along which the role of the Church will be most fruitfully investigated in future. At a time when the relationships of the various ministries within the Church to each other are undergoing readjustment in view of the doctrinal insights regained at Vatican II (collegiality, charismatic nature of the Church, etc.), it is well to remind ourselves of the message and ministry of the whole Church. In this way necessary perspective will be retained on what are primarily internal questions. At the same time we must remember that the manner in which internal questions are settled, and this applies especially to the exercise of collegiality at all levels in the Church, will affect the image and credibility of the Church as a whole. What is particularly required of us at the present time is that we should not in our enthusiasm for new discoveries – however valid they may be – underrate the value of what is traditional and established. For this reason we shall begin with a brief word on the role of the papacy (in the context, though, of our general topic as already described), in the interests of preserving a balanced outlook at the present time of debate and discussion.

The Papacy

The promulgation of *Humanae Vitae* brought a fairly sharp reaction from many people who felt that its net result would be to diminish the authority and credibility of the papal office. Observers at Lambeth 1968 inform us of the chilled reaction of many of the bishops who saw in the encyclical evidence of the irrelevance of what the Church had to say to the modern world and of the Pope's insensitivity to the over-population problem.[2] Without wishing to take any stand on the correctness or opportuneness of *Humanae Vitae*, we may say that to base one's estimate of the papal attitude to over-population on it alone, is less than fair even if there is some justification for it. One must not forget that Pope Paul also wrote *Populorum Progressio*. The Lambeth bishops saw in the manner in which *Humanae Vitae* was issued a 'blow to collegiality' and in this view there is much justification. In fact the rather hesitant and unsure exercise of collegiality which we are now experiencing *post eventum*, would not have been necessary if adequate consultation with the universal episcopate had taken place before the encyclical was issued. What is quite clear is that we are witnessing a modification in practice of the papal style of teaching in moral matters. Here again we would urge the necessity of maintaining a correct balance. It is a matter of doing justice to the papal teaching office and to collegiality at the same time. We are speaking now only of the present concrete historical form of the papal primacy; the personal infallibility, supreme magisterium and primacy of jurisdiction of the Pope are not in

2. These criticisms occurred during discussions and were not reflected in the Resolutions adopted. Cf. John Coventry, S.J. (who was an observer at the Conference), in *The Month*, November 1968 especially p. 266.

question since they are neither being appealed to nor denied in the present discussion.

Catholics who tend to undervalue the papacy or who see in it an insuperable obstacle to reunion at the present time would do well to ponder the words of the well-known Episcopalian priest and New Testament scholar Dr Frederick Grant who wrote recently as follows of the papal office:

> For all its failings in the past, for all its blunders and mistakes, and the folly of a few selfish, self-seeking, or cowardly men, the general course and aim of the (papal) institution has been forward and upward. Far from discarding it, or disregarding it, and in spite of the false claims often made for it, and the flimsy exegesis its apologists have too often employed, the papacy is one of the most priceless elements in the Christian heritage. Reformed and restored to a pristine state ... the papacy might very well become the acknowledged leader, guide and chief of the whole Christian Church, and the greatest influence for good in all the world.[3]

This is a weighty claim, particularly from an Episcopalian priest who is by no means about to become a Catholic. And yet anyone who is familiar, for example, with the social teaching of the Catholic Church as expressed in the great encyclicals from *Rerum Novarum* issued by Leo XIII in 1891 down to *Populorum Progressio* issued by Pope Paul in 1967 will concede that Dr Grant's claim is justifiable.

Indeed, it is one of the most regrettable features of nineteenth- and twentieth-century Catholic history that papal social teaching has frequently been ignored both by bishops and by businessmen and industrialists. Part of the reason for this phenomenon (which has been one of the factors leading to the loss of large numbers of the working classes belonging to the European Church) may lie in the fact that some Catholics tend to be

3. Frederick Grant, *Rome and Reunion*, Oxford 1965, 144.

excessively preoccupied with the formal authority attaching to papal pronouncements and not sufficiently occupied with the intrinsic weight and value which derives from the importance of the subject matter itself. There is a tendency either to say, 'this teaching is infallible and must be given the assent of faith' or to adopt the attitude, 'this teaching is non-infallible and consequently may be ignored or merely deferred to'. In fact, since the nineteenth century only two papal proclamations are surely known to be infallible: the dogmas of the Immaculate Conception and the Assumption. But this does not mean that the non-infallible but authentic teaching of the pope may be politely ignored as has been done *when that teaching concerned social matters.*

The dogmatic encyclicals of the popes, on the contrary, in recent years have been widely acclaimed and have been influential. Clearly these latter are not irreformable as Vatican II has shown with reference to *Mystici Corporis* and its teaching on the identity between the Mystical Body and the Roman Catholic Church (to take but one example). Even though Pope John taught that Catholic social doctrine is an integral part of the Christian conception of life it has never exercised the same influence as have the doctrinal encyclicals. We are not suggesting that doctrinal and social encyclicals are on quite the same level in the assent they require even though both alike are reformable. The ignoring of the Church's social teaching by Catholics must be due, in part, to the mentality which 'privatized religion' and made it an affair of personal salvation.[4] Social thought was radically separated from moral, dogmatic or scriptural theology and the social and cosmic consequences of redemption were neglected.

Analysis of the development of Catholic social teaching from Leo XIII down to Pope Paul VI would take us too far afield. We merely wish to emphasize the part the papacy has played in

4. See J. B. Metz, 'Relationship of Church and World in the Light of a Political Theology', *Theology of Renewal, Vol. II Renewal of Religious Structures,* N.Y. 1968, 257.

showing the relevance and value of the Christian faith in the political, economic and industrial fields, and all the while in defence of the rights and dignity of the human person and in the interests of peace and justice.

Perhaps the high point in this papal effort was reached under Pope John XXIII and with the issuing of *Pacem in Terris* in 1963. It is instructive to recall the comments made at that time by Karl Barth since they concern the papal office and its style of teaching and not merely, therefore, the personal charismatic exercise of power by John XXIII. Impressed by the impact made on the world by *Pacem in Terris,* despite the fact that prior to Pope John other Church leaders had expressed themselves on human rights, the problems of race, minorities, refugees and colonialism, the task of the United Nations, atomic and general disarmament, Barth asked:

> But why is it that the voice of Rome made such a far greater impression than the voice of Geneva on the world (from the editor's desk of *Pravda* all the way to that of the *Basler Nationalzeitung*)? Was it only because of the obviously greater historical and political halo which Rome possesses? Is the reason not also the fact that in the encyclical the same things were not only talked about but also *proclaimed*, that Christianity and the world were not only taught but summoned unreservedly and bindingly with an equal appeal to the highest authority, that they received not only advice and admonition but also directives, in short, that the encyclical had more the character of a *message* than our previous ecumenical proclamations, in spite of its extensive use of concepts taken from natural law?[5]

It is noteworthy that when Vatican II assembled, one of its

5. Karl Barth, 'Thoughts on the Second Vatican Council', in *New Theology No. 1,* edited by Martin E. Marty and Dean G. Pearman, New York 1964, 118.

first official acts was to issue a *Message to Humanity*.[6] Karl Barth would probably have approved its strongly biblical flavour. The theme of the Message is the self-renewal of the Church and the presentation by this renewed Church of God's truth in its fullness and beauty to the world so that men may understand and accept it. The style of papal teaching which Barth praised so highly was adopted also by the Church in the *Pastoral Constitution on the Church in the Modern World* in which the Church enters into dialogue with the modern world.[7]

The Pastoral Constitution on the Church in the Modern World contains a synthesis, development and extension of the papal social teaching since 1891. But it was written during the Council when a definite growth in self-awareness was achieved by the Church and a much more complete and nuanced theology of the world and secular realities was developed as well. We shall turn, therefore, to the documents of Vatican II but principally to the *Pastoral Constitution on the Church in the Modern World* in order to see what the Church has to offer to mankind by way of guidance for living today. We shall examine briefly the Church's awareness of her own nature in her conversation with the world; her concept of 'the world'; how she views their mutual relationship and what she has to preach – or proclaim by her very existence – to the world today.

The Church's Self-awareness in Dialogue

We are not attempting to present an abbreviated doctrine of the Church here: all that is said in the *Dogmatic Constitution on the Church* and in other places about the nature of the Church is presupposed. We shall select the aspects which are relevant to our present purpose. What is omitted is neither denied nor ignored.

When engaging in conversation with the world the Church

6. See W. M. Abbott (ed.), *The Documents of Vatican II*, New York 1966, 3-7.

7. *Ibid.*, 199-308. Subsequent references as follows: C.M.W., with number of article.

describes herself as a mysterious communion of God and men united in Christ through the power of the holy Spirit. This Church is a pilgrim people journeying towards the kingdom of God meanwhile *manifesting* that God's love for man, as definitively expressed in Christ, is truly and really present in the Church for the world, and *exercising* that love through faith, hope and charity.

The Church – being the community of those who have welcomed the gospel – regards herself as having one essential purpose, which is to bring about the salvation of the whole human race – and not, therefore, of her own members only. The Church is structured in a certain way: she possesses word and sacrament, an authoritative teaching body and a creed but she is aware that none of these is an end in itself. The Church is a sign pointing to the 'kingdom of God', but she is also aware that this kingdom, though yet to be fulfilled, is a present but hidden reality in herself – the Church is *sacrament* and sign.

As a visible society the Church is the expression of the victory achieved by the risen Christ. This relationship with the risen Christ is a frequent theme in the Council documents and has important implications in a Church also conscious of being a pilgrim Church always in need of renewal, always developing and – now – frequently changing where change is appropriate and necessary.

The Church regards all her structures and endowments as existing to subserve the transforming action of Christ which takes place in the individual in his total persona, social and cosmic environment. The Church recognizes, too, that God's grace has always been active in the world from the beginning of history down to the present time when this grace is redemptively active outside the visible limits of the Church both among those who practise forms of religion other than the Christian and even among those 'who in shadow and images seek the unknown God'. Because of the universal will to save of almighty God the Church knows of the possibility of salvation for those who are not formally her members. But she knows that saving grace is mediated to men through the Church. She is 'the universal sacrament of salvation' continuing Christ's work of achieving true communion of men with God and with each other visibly and effectively, invisibly and really, through her own instrumentality.[8]

The Church today professes her awareness that she is not primarily an object to be *known*. She is a reality to be lived and experienced connaturally by the believing member whose experience of the Church in faith will precede and exceed his clear conceptual clarification of what is a mysterious communion.

The Church has an eschatological aspect. The kingdom present in her in mystery will be brought to full flower when the Lord comes (C.M.W., art. 39). Here and now to believe in God revealed in Christ is already to share in future glory; faith is the beginning of salvation and the source of justification. But the Church is fully incarnate in the world: real Church in real world just as her founder was real God and real man and so salvation is not a question of faith or attitudes or commitment only. The Church is aware of temporal realities in all their daily and concrete particularity and she is aware that no amount of concern for an ultimate destiny will excuse from the everyday task to reach after the true and the good and to overcome all forms of selfishness in giving oneself to others.

The kingdom to which the Church is directed is eschatological: it is not the achievement of a thoroughly Christian civilization on earth much less a super-welfare state which ushers in the kingdom of God. And yet the Christian programme of achieving the Christian ideal and of achieving the consecration of the world must go on. This does not always mean 'Christianizing'. There is such a thing as 'emancipating' the world to its intrinsic secularity which may be a Christian task.[9]

---

8. C.M.W., art. 45. For an excellent commentary on the *Dogmatic Constitution on the Church* cf. Kevin McNamara (ed.), *Vatican II: The Constitution on the Church: A Theological and Pastoral Commentary*, Dublin 1968.

9. Cf. Karl Rahner, 'Church and World', in *Sacramentum Mundi I*, London 1968, 346-56.

The World

The Church addresses her message to living men to 'all men of good will' in Pope John's phrase. But it is the human family in its total environment which is addressed. We might say man in his personal, social and cosmic dimensions to safeguard the idea that while it is man and the totality of his relationships (familial, social and political) which are in question, created realities are not excluded as irrelevant. Four different historical stages of the world appear to be envisaged and we shall deal with each of these separately.

(a) *The World as Created*

The Church frequently recalls the familiar doctrine of creation: God made the world out of nothing and saw that it was very good (*Gen.* 1:31). Important implications of this doctrine are the *dependence* of all created reality (personal and other) – the creature is unintelligible without the creator – and the *intrinsic goodness* and *value* of the temporal order which provide the basis for recognizing the proper autonomy of earthly affairs. The doctrine of creation must not be misunderstood as though it described an activity which took place in the past and is of historical interest only. The primary emphasis in the doctrine is on the present: we are creatures who exist in a state of dependence on God. Creation refers also to the future, to what we were created to become. Since this concerns our glorification in and with Christ our attention should be focused on Christ and our future glory and not on Adam and the state from which man supposedly fell.[10]

There is the further point concerning created things as providing natural revelation of God who, through his Word, created all that is. When the Council asserts that God gives men an enduring witness of himself through the things that are made there is no question of wishing to recapture the wrong sense of awe or superstition where nature is concerned. But neither will

10. Cf. A. Hulsbosch, *God in Creation and Evolution,* New York 1965.

the Church allow the deist concept of nature – created and then abandoned to run its course – to prevail. In this way the true dignity and worth of nature are preserved and man's steward-ship – *responsible* use of created realities – is suggested.

(b) *The World as Fallen*

The Council states that personal sin which man committed at the promptings of 'personified evil' caused disorder at the per-sonal, social and cosmic levels (by cosmic here is meant 'all created things'). By stressing the created nature of the world and then by insisting that sin is historical the Council is safe-guarding against the idea that to be *creature* is *thereby* to be *fallen*. Sin – and the evil consequences which result from it in man himself and in his social relationships – is the result of man's being free. The implications of this are that any form of dualism which would regard evil as a necessary part of the very structure of reality is absolutely excluded. At times the Council documents read as if the Church were still carrying on a con-scious struggle with dualism. A further implication of her teach-ing on the world as fallen appears to be that since some social ills come not merely from underdevelopment or less sophisti-cated social structures but also are the effects of sin (and fre-quently, of course, the cause of further sin) knowledge of the fact of sin is imperative if man is to treat of social problems adequately (C.M.W., art. 13).

(c) *The World as Redeemed*

The fallen world was not abandoned by God who offered men 'helps to salvation' in anticipation of Christ. But it was Christ who broke the grip of 'personified evil' on the world and set it free. The full implications of the redemption of the world by Christ as this is presented in Vatican II will not be worked out for a considerable length of time yet. But we can indicate some important directions which this teaching has taken particularly in the *Pastoral Constitution on the Church in the Modern World*, where it is presented as part of the Church's understanding of the world.

We have already mentioned the fact that the Church acknowledges the existence and redeeming effects of grace outside her own visible (and temporal) boundaries. Redeeming grace, however, where it exists is mediated through the Church and possesses an inherent dynamism towards the Church. In this sense salvation is from the Church. What is noteworthy about the *Pastoral Constitution on the Church in the Modern World,* is the manner in which it develops the relationship of every man to Christ and to the paschal mystery by which the world was saved.

The mystery which every man is is illuminated by the mystery of the incarnate Word who 'united himself in some fashion' with every man by the Incarnation and also by his fully human life of thought, love and action. The Christian man is transformed in a special way in the likeness of Christ dying and rising and this transformation takes place through the Christian link with the paschal mystery. But, the Council asserts, every man in whom grace is at work is, through the holy Spirit, offered the possibility of being associated with the paschal mystery.[11]

(d) *The World to be Fulfilled*

The redemptive work of Christ has already decided the destiny of the world in favour of salvation and victory. This outcome, although irrevocably achieved, is hidden and is known only by faith. This phase of the world's history might be referred to as its 'eschatological era'. Once again the central concern of the Council is man the concrete individual in his total set of social, economic, political – and other – relationships, but the total environment which includes created realities is also envisaged. The doctrines of creation and redemption and the Church's sacramental system make clear that the redeeming work of

11. C.M.W., art. 22; cf. *Dogmatic Constitution on the Church,* art. 2, 8, etc.

Christ which is continued in the Church has implications for created realities.

Repeatedly the assertion occurs in the Council documents that the Christian must take responsibility for constructing the temporal order. The task is envisaged in two stages: the task of the right establishment of the temporal order, and in this all men should cooperate, and the task of directing it to God through Christ, which is the specific Christian contribution.[12]

The 'temporal order' is the name given to the whole complex of scientific, cultural, economic, academic, political – national and international – and other professional or vocational pursuits in which man engages. It is pointed out that these possess proper intrinsic value – they are not, then, to be used as means to an end – even to the ultimate end which is salvation – in such a way that their intrinsic value is disregarded.[13]

Thus, while the Church is at pains to show that the temporal order derives special dignity from the fact that it is designed to serve the human person, it is also at pains to emphasize the intrinsic strength and excellence of the temporal order which is enhanced by the ultimate orientation of all things to Christ (*Col.* 1:18).

Realistically, the Council recognizes the potential evil of created realities but it points out that the source of their possible misuse – which can result in 'corruption of morals and human institutions and not rarely in contempt for the human person himself' – lies in the effects which sin has on man's knowledge of God, man and the moral law. It is not said that there is a *necessary* connection between the growth in autonomy of secular realities and their (sinful) misuse by man.[14]

The impression must not be given that there is any improper suspicion of the world – of the temporal order – in the Council documents. On the contrary the continuity between engaging

12. Cf. *Decree on the Apostolate of the Laity*, art. 5-8; C.M.W., art. 93 etc.
13. Cf. *Decree on the Apostolate of the Laity*, art. 7.
14. *Ibid.*

fully in the temporal task and being genuinely religious is stressed. In fact the Council comes very near to an anathema when it declares roundly that there must be 'no false opposition between professional and social activities on the one part, and religious life on the other. *The Christian who neglects his temporal duties neglects his duties toward his neighbour and even God, and jeopardizes his eternal salvation.*' The split between faith and daily life is regarded by the Council as one of the 'most serious of contemporary errors' (C.M.W., art. 43, italics added).

Relationship between Church and World

The Church is in the world but not of the world. It constitutes an order of salvation prepared by the Father, accomplished by the Son, perfected and renewed by the holy Spirit. The Church is from God. It is not a human creation. The distinction between the Church and the world is clarified by saying that the *specific purpose* of the Church is salvation, that is the supernatural communion of all men with each other in God (C.M.W., art. 45).

When speaking of the relationship between Church and world the Council is careful to avoid giving the idea of a society existing over against the world. The Council speaks of the Church *in* the world – but not at home in it – and so it becomes a question of clarifying and enriching our understanding of *how* the Church is in the world.

Any clear-cut and simplified account of how the Church is in the world is avoided but many valuable insights are afforded. The Church is a community of men intimately linked with the human community. She is present in the world as 'a kind of soul for human society' or as 'leaven is in bread', that is, animating society with the spirit and life of Christ. The relationship of the Church to the world is in fact a mystery which can be penetrated by faith but which is also kept in disarray by sin and will be until the coming of the kingdom. The different stages of the world's history which are distinguished for the sake of clarity are not neatly divided historical periods one of which ends when the other begins: there is continuity and over-lapping. We should beware of 'reifying' the concept of the world: it is primarily man and personal sin which are in question. The results of sin – social and political evils – do assume a supra-personal force and the Council refers explicitly to 'personified evil' but there is no question of any form of dualism especially with reference to material creation (C.M.W., art. 40).

The Church is hopeful that from her self-renewal men will receive enlightenment about their true nature and vocation and also she is hopeful that from her spiritual self-renewal will come a 'happy impulse on behalf of human values such as scientific discoveries, technological advances, and a wider diffusion of knowledge'.[15] Conscious of her primarily spiritual nature the Church is aware of intangible but real influence exercised by her on human institutions: she speaks of *function, light* and *energy* in this connection and is aware that she can powerfully influence human society for the better (C.M.W., art. 42).

The Church is also conscious that she is an independent, self-governing society which serves man in his personal and social being, and yet on the basis of a right and purpose which differ from those of the state.[16] The Church maintains her freedom to preach the faith, teach her social doctrine, and her right of intervention to judge and condemn in matters concerning the political order whenever personal rights or moral issues are at stake (C.M.W., art. 76). However, the Church desires peaceful coexistence and cooperation with all men. She explicitly disclaims having received any proper mission from Christ in the political, economic, or social order and reiterates that her purpose is salvation. But she is interested in the person in all his community relationships and for that reason she stresses the intrinsic connection between human activities and religion. She is real Church in real world and reserves the right to initiate

15. *Message to Humanity, op. cit.,* p. 5.
16. Cf. *Dogmatic Constitution on the Church,* art. 8; C.M.W., art. 44.

directly, services for the benefit of the poor and the needy (C.M.W., art. 42).

A frequent theme in the Council documents is that the Church wishes to imitate Christ in his service of humanity and this idea dominates in the Church's awareness of her presence in the world. She is there to serve, not to dominate or dictate.[17] The Church, as we have already indicated, seeks no self-aggrandizement – or should not – since she does not exist for her own sake. She points beyond herself to the 'kingdom of God' where her hope is fixed and her full realization lies.

The Church freely acknowledges, today, that she has been and is enriched in her missionary task by developments which have taken place in human history, in philosophy and in the sciences. She is assisted by such developments in her reflection on and deeper understanding of her own (mysterious) nature and of the continuing necessity of appropriate change and adaptation to changing times and circumstances (C.M.W., art. 44).

The Message of the Church

The primary 'message' proclaimed by the Church to the modern world comes from what the Church is and does rather than from what she says in the sense of a manifesto or code for behaviour. The Church exists to praise God and to sanctify men. She exists to proclaim salvation and to enact the work of salvation which is proclaimed. This the Church does most effectively through the liturgy where Christ does it through the Church. 'By Baptism men are plunged into the paschal mystery of Christ – they die with him, are buried with him and rise with him' (*Constitution on the Sacred Liturgy,* art. 6.). And in the liturgy the Word of God is preached and the death of Christ is proclaimed until he returns. Men's sins are forgiven, the presence of God's truth and love with men, and their response in faith, hope and charity, are deepened and intensiefid. To do and proclaim all this is the primary function of the Church.

17. C.M.W., art. 3; see also *Dogmatic Constitution on the Church,* art. 32.

Has the Church no message, then, for the modern world beyond the witness given by her own life at its most intense point, its Christian summit? The Church has a profound mess- age for the world and it consists essentially in reminding the world of God's truth which concerns creation, fall, redemption, fulfilment.

The Church reads the 'signs of the times' carefully. She is aware of the magnificence and misery of the modern world. She perceives that the technological and scientific advances of modern man serve to raise ever more sharply the inescapable human questions: what is man? and what is the meaning of human existence? She perceives modern man still baffled by death and sorrow and sin and yet standing on the threshold of a new era when he may literally determine the future of the world and of himself. Of course man has always determined his future by the free actions of his present but this has been a case of making his own soul. Man's free decisions have shaped the course of history – determined the future – but today science has put qualitatively different power to change in man's hands. It is to this man that the Church addresses herself in conversation.

She does not pretend to have all the answers to the 'problem' set to her by modern man. Rather she sets out to illuminate a mystery in the light of the gospel (C.M.W., art. 10). And the first part of the message – man is a mystery – must not be lost sight of. The Church's gospel is: the key to the understand- ing of all human life and striving, its goal and focal point is Jesus Christ dead and risen again. Man is a mystery, he becomes a riddle or an absurd bafflement to himself apart from Christ and the light and strength of the Spirit of Christ.

The Church points beyond herself to Christ in his present state of victory and glory and she tells man that in the reality (name) of Christ and in him alone is man's salvation. But in preaching the Christ of glory the Church points backward in time to a real man who 'worked with human hands, thought with a human mind, acted by human choice and loved with a human heart', a man who shared the sinful human condition, was tempted but did not sin. The Church points to a vivid man of his times who was indignant, angry, who healed and forgave, who dedicated himself to serve, to be humble, to be despised and outcast and to die. He was sent as 'a man to man' to reveal to men the innermost realities about God by what he said and did but especially through his death and resurrection and his sending of the holy Spirit. And she proclaims to man today that only in this life, in thinking of it, in following its spirit, but above all in coming into life-giving contact with it, will man begin to understand the mystery that he is and begin to learn to create the universal brotherhood that he ultimately desires. The Church preaches the mystery of Christ but she also tells man that he, too, is a mystery which takes on light only in the mystery of the Word made flesh (C.M.W., art. 22, etc.).

The Meaning of Life

It is significant that when the Church faces today the question of the meaning of man and of human existence she replies by reaffirming the doctrine of creation, or rather the gospel of creation in conjunction with the gospel of redemption and it has been said that no combination of ideas is more important for biblical faith than the continued affirmation that God is not only redeemer but creator as well.[18] The Church tells man that he is created in the image of God, that he is the centre and crown to whom all other things are related, that he is appointed to be the one who will master, subdue and use all other created things for God's glory. She reminds man that he was not created solitary but that he is a social being by his very nature and she reminds him that marriage is the primary form of interpersonal communion (C.M.W., art. 12). Now these affirmations may appear trite, but on the contrary, in the context in which they occur they are of profound significance. The Church knows that it has been entrusted to her to reveal the mystery of God, but

18. Langdon Gilkey, *Maker of Heaven and Earth. The Christian Doctrine of Creation in the Light of Modern Knowledge,* New York 1958, 1.

God is the origin and goal of man and so if the Church is to open up to man the innermost truth about himself and the meaning of his own existence she must tell him of his creature-hood, that he is from God and for God and that the deepest longings of his heart will never be satisfied by anything created but only by God himself.

Secondly, in repeating the doctrine of creation the Church is affirming the goodness of the created order, of man himself and of man's activity in constructing the temporal order. The idea that salvation is offered to the soul alone is forever laid to rest; the whole man, the entire world are proffered hope and fulfil-ment. The doctrine of creation is fundamental to the assurance that life has meaning and purpose, and this is why the first article of the Creed contains profession of faith in *God the Father almighty, Creator of heaven and earth*. This is why, too, the answer 'God made the world' used to be the first answer in our catechisms.

Perhaps the implications of the doctrine of creation had begun to escape us because we were not taking the problem of evil seriously enough. This is a charge which cannot be levelled at very many today when extremely sharp consciousness of evil in its social and political manifestations is found. Famine, increasing mental illness, the threat of war with possible total annihilation ... enough manifestations of evil to pose the prob-lem of God in its most acute form. There is no need to repeat the dilemmas which have been posed for theists by those who felt that the intensity of evil in the world proved either the non-existence of God, or his impotence, or lack of concern, if he did exist. Today, many feel they have 'no need of the God hypo-thesis' because they believe that science and technology have made it possible for man to eradicate evil completely from the world. Science appears to be on the verge of discovering the secrets of the origins of the universe and the 'God of explana-tion' is no longer required. In the past the dualistic heresy led to fatalism in the face of evil which was regarded as a necessary and ineradicable feature of the universe. This was so because evil was regarded as originating in an evil principle standing eternally in opposition to God and limiting him. Today, starting from the facts of social evil and human misery, some are led to assert as a moral absolute the principle that evil has no right to exist. It cannot be tolerated, and since this is what God appears to do God must be rejected. In Courtney Murray's words, man rejects God in the name of his own more God-like morality.[19] Thus the problem of evil, belief in the human capacity to eradicate it, and forms of atheism go together. To all such forms of atheism, whatever their source, and to all tendencies to despair and anxiety in the face of evil and suffering (and these are really encountered as responses to the problem of evil; not everyone shares the optimism that man will conquer evil, and in the absence of belief in God despair results) the Church reaffirms the doctrines of the creation and fall of man, and the doctrine of the fall is also necessary if man is to understand his present condition and his own limitations in approaching the problem of evil, which is more than merely natural in its source and dimensions. 'Sin has caused a cleavage in human life which runs right through all that is human.'[20] The Council rightly sees in ignorance of sin the basis for a new form of idolatry in which excessive confidence is placed in scientific advances; science may alleviate many human hardships but it cannot save from sin. Along with her reaffirmation of the doctrine of creation the Church replies, too, with the witness of lives where confidence and serenity are found in the face of evil, sin and suffering, a confidence born of faith, hope and love which are possible in the last analysis because of man's assurance that the ultimate reality is all wise, all good and all powerful, and has communicated its own truth and power to love, to man.

The Church's doctrine of man as expressed in her dialogue

19. John C. Murray, *The Problem of God*, Yale University Press 1965, 108.
20. Emil Brunner, *The Divine Imperative: A Study in Christian Ethics*, London 1964, 62.

with the world repeats the facts of his creatureliness, the intrinsic goodness of his body, the existence of his soul and the central importance of conscience and its freedom in man's moral and religious life. All forms of dualism and tendencies towards angelism or materialism are avoided. The Church stresses that man is social of his very nature, and appeals, in a brief allusion, to the doctrine of the blessed Trinity in explanation of the fact that man can only fully find himself through a sincere gift of himself (C.M.W., art. 24). This analogy between the human person – its profound need for and tendency towards communion – and the blessed Trinity, is seen as basic to the fundamental unity of the love of God and the love of neighbour which together are referred to as the 'first and greatest commandment'. The inadequacy of a merely individualistic ethic and the need for a communitarian ethic may ultimately be traced to his dynamism towards communion in man who is the image of the Triune God (C.M.W., art. 30).

It is significant that marriage is described as the 'primary form of interpersonal communion' since the Church's constant theme in the Council is that her efforts in self-renewal and preaching the gospel are to make life more human, and that there is continuity between her religious task and man's secular task. Making life more human must mean making it more personal today. Marriage is regarded as the first and vital cell of society. It is also the 'domestic Church', or the Church in miniature, in Rahner's phrase. For the Church, marriage is a natural institution and a sacrament. It was instituted by the creator, and sanctified in a special way by Christ of whose union with the Church it is the mysterious sign and symbol (C.M.W., art. 47-52). Thus through sanctifying marriage and through making of it a true communion of love, faith and hope, the first and one of the most important steps is already taken by the Church in her task of humanizing and penetrating with her sanctifying influence the larger social and political societies. In the Church's relationship to the family, in her concern that marriage should be a true covenant of love, her mission and

possibilities for the modern world are brought into sharpest
focus.

As regards the larger political societies and national and
international problems the Church, while she has much to say,
has no specific programme, policy or ideology for the solution
of political or economic problems. And yet it seems eminently
sensible to say that there is room for what one theologian calls
'political theology', especially to counteract the tendency easily
fostered by personalist and existential-oriented theology (which
has its merits, too) to reduce religion to the situation of the
individual alone before God. Religion does involve placing the
individual in a position of decision and responsibility before
God, but, as the Council reminded us, man is social of his very
nature, and men and their associations must cultivate the moral
and social virtues and work for their promotion in society.
'Political theology seeks to make contemporary theologians
aware that a trial is pending between the eschatological message
of Jesus and the socio-political reality. It insists on the permanent relation to the world inherent in the salvation merited by
Jesus, a relation not to be understood in a natural-cosmological
but in a socio-political sense: that is, as a critical, liberating
force in regard to the social world and its historical process.'[21]

Message and Laws

Our insistence on the Church's message as a proclamation of
the gospel and a reaffirmation of the Church's age-old doctrines,
which are new only in their relevance and significance to the
often unrecognized but truly religious questions of the day, must
not be taken to imply that the Church has abdicated her role as
authoritative teacher of morality. On the contrary, the gospel
proclaimed by the Church knows of an immutable moral law
the precepts of which are and will be taught irreformably by the
Church. This is the divine law which is acknowledged by man
through the mediation of his conscience. The divine law is associated with the divine wisdom and is eternal, objective and

21. Metz, *art. cit.*, 261.

universal. That the divine law is asserted to be objective is important in that it safeguards against a mere ethic of inspiration as though morality were a matter of the intensity of personal commitment and not of objective right and wrong. In view of the many changes taking place in the Church today it is well to stress that she regards the divine law as immutable because of its relationship to God and his eternal wisdom, and not because of any positive (and hence mutable) decisions of the Church. The Church not merely proclaims a universal, objective, divine law, she claims the right to declare that certain concrete actions are right or wrong on the basis, ultimately, of this law. The divine law and the natural law, over which the Church claims competence, are not merely formal principles; they have content as well and the Church is quite specific in declaring, for example, that divorce and adultery are evil and that the rights of the human person are absolute and inviolable. It is clear, from her profound conviction that the highest norm for human life is the divine law in which man has been made to participate by God, that the Church regards the teaching of principles of morality as an integral and indispensable part of her mandate to teach man God's truth in its fullness.

However, the Church recognizes limits to the amount of detailed, concrete direction which she can or should give to men in their lives and work. The limits here apply to the hierarchy, or to the magisterium, since the Church clearly recognizes circumstances when laymen, for example, in the light of the gospel and the principles of morality, will be called on to make concrete decisions on the basis of their own responsibility and not as a result of teaching received from the hierarchy.[22] Explicitly

22. C.M.W., art. 76: 'It is highly important, especially in pluralistic societies, that a proper view exist of the relation between the political communiy and the Church. Thus the faithful will be able to make a clear distinction between what Christian conscience leads them to do in their own name as citizens, whether as individuals or in association, and what they do in the name of the Church and in union with her shepherds. Cf. *Decree on the Apostolate of the Laity*, art. 24, 31.

excluded is the idea that the layman's 'pastors are always such experts, that to every problem which arises, however complicated, they can readily give him a concrete solution, or even that such is their mission. Rather, enlightened by Christian wisdom and giving close attention to the teaching authority of the Church, let the layman take on his own distinctive role.' We are told that frequently the Christian view of things will provide – 'suggest' is the word used – a concrete solution in certain circumstances, the implication being that sometimes it will not (C.M.W., art. 43). Thus the Church is admitting in a wider context what she has always acknowledged at the personal level – in the choice of a vocation in life, or of a marriage partner – that there is an area of human decision and action where personal conscience alone is competent. This is not the same thing as saying that morality is ultimately subjective, or that all moral decisions are fundamentally personally made and hence not authoritatively imposed (which is true); rather, it has to do with an inherent limit which appertains to universal moral principles in certain concrete cases where the application of the principle does not terminate in one, and only one, course of action.[23]

The Church is led to this admission by her deeper understanding of her own fundamental role as 'sacrament' and mediator of universal salvation, by her awareness of the presence of the Spirit in all the faithful, by her recognition of the primacy of personal, conscientious decision, and especially by consciousness of the complexity of modern life where the distance between universal principles and their application in the concrete has frequently increased considerably, so that the same certainty or ease no longer accompany the making of concrete decisions.

23. We have only touched on questions of fundamental importance regarding the relationship between universal norms and concrete decisions. Our intention is to show that certain positions were adopted at the Council; full analysis and theoretical justification belong elsewhere, cf. Rahner, *The Christian of the Future*, London 1966, and also his many writings on situation ethics and what he calls the 'formal existential ethic' for fuller discussion of the problems involved.

There is the further recognition of the legitimate autonomy of secular pursuits and the growing realization by the Church that 'emancipating the world to its own proper secularity' far from being an undesirable, new form of paganism is a Christian task and is a consequence of a true religious understanding of the world rather than a denial of it.[24]

The Church today is not unconcerned with moral principles or their clear enunciation but – and this is quite another matter – one notices in the Council documents an unwillingness to prescribe particular, concrete courses of action for today's vast and complex problems. Noticeably present is the tendency for the magisterium to take seriously the idea that the Church, like the individual, is historical and must grow in the knowledge of the truth in the light of developing and rapidly changing situations. The very debates carried out in the Aula on specific issues – like birth-regulation, in so far as it was discussed, and the morality of nuclear warfare – were sufficient to convince the bishops that the Church has no privileged or easy access to the truth concerning the morality of such issues.

What then has the Church to offer where the role of detailed, definitive guidance in moral matters is eschewed? Rahner says that in such circumstances the Church would need to give the individual three things: '(1) A more living ardour of Christian inspiration as a basis of individual life; (2) an absolute conviction that the moral responsibility of the individual is not at an end because he does not come in conflict with any concrete instruction of the official Church; (3) an initiation into the holy art of finding the concrete prescriptions for his own decision in the call of God, in other words, the logic of concrete particular decision which of course does justice to universal regulative principles but cannot wholly be deduced from them solely by explicit casuistry'.[25]

In her pastoral mission the Church claims the right to lay

---

24. Cf. Rahner, 'Church and World', in *Sacramentum Mundi I*.
25. Rahner, *The Christian of the Future*, 46-7.

down positive legal prescriptions and to require from her members obedience to them as a matter of duty. However, the distinction between such enactments (e.g., it is wrong to vote Communist in this election) and laws which clearly express or apply divine laws must be carefully preserved. When the Church imposes positive legal prescriptions she must do so with the understanding that judgements of inexpediency or inopportuneness may be expressed by members of the laity qualified to judge in such matters. Such judgements, when expressed, must not be equated with disobedience to divine law. The Council documents maintain the right of the Church to make binding prescriptions for the spiritual good of her members. The only thing constant about this right is the right itself: no individual exercise of the right as expressed in positive human law can be considered immutable and irreformable.

The Church today not only reassures man about the meaning and value of human life with reference to the creative-redemptive work of God. She also endorses the view (which is as old as Genesis) that man, made in the image of the 'creating God' is himself a 'co-creator', that as the Council has it, with the help of grace man can be recreated himself and become the artisan of a new humanity. The Church's message to mankind contains much that is valuable in terms of man's duty to build a better world. This is not to say that a detailed plan for the future is offered. The Church has no such detailed plan. What the Church knows about the future is essentially that it has already begun to exist in the risen Christ who is the pledge and the goal of man's future and who, through his Spirit, is leading man to his true future which is the Father. The Church insists on man's task to heal and construct the temporal order. She insists, too, that her own teaching on man's future destiny must not be allowed to diminish man's interest in, or his responsibility for, the future which he is called on to create. Rather, she insists, her teaching on the promises which the future holds undergirds man's performance of his earthly task with the incentives and hope which are indispensable if man is to persevere in his task.

In effect, the Church warns man against absolutizing any human future which he may produce and which in many respects may be very good, by reiterating that man is made for God and that the essence of idolatry consists in substituting something less in the place of God. Any man-made future will always be 'something less'. To say this is not to reduce man's attitude to the future to one of patient, passive expectation. Once again there is not a question of a choice of opposites: God's future or man's self-made future. There is question instead of synthesis, continuity and transcendence. The future is God's grace and man's task. We work at the building and creation of a future 'of which God himself is the dynamism'.[26] The essence of the Church's message to the modern world is to remind man that his earthly task is of vital concern to the kingdom of God but must not be identified with that kingdom.

'For after we have obeyed the Lord, and in his Spirit nurtured on earth the values of human dignity, brotherhood and freedom, and indeed all the good fruits of our nature and enterprise, we will find them again, but freed of stain, burnished and trans-figured. This will be so when Christ hands over to the Father a kingdom eternal and universal: "a kingdom of truth and life, of holiness and grace, of justice, love, and peace". On this earth that kingdom is already present in mystery. When the Lord returns, it will be brought into full flower' (C.M.W., art. 39).

26. Cf. J. B. Metz, 'The Church and the World', in *The World in History: The St Xavier Symposium*, edited by T. Patrick Burke, New York 1966.